THE THEORY AND PRACTICE OF VIRTUE

Michael G. Whitzah
Milwaukee
14. XI. 1986

The Theory and Practice of Virtue

GILBERT C. MEILAENDER

University of Notre Dame Press
Notre Dame, Indiana 46556

Library of Congress Cataloging in Publication Data

Meilaender, Gilbert, 1946-
The theory and practice of virtue.

Includes bibliographical references and index.
1. Virtue–Addresses, essays, lectures. I. Title.
BJ1521.M55   1984   179'.9   83-40598
ISBN 0-268-01852-9

Manufactured in the United States of America

TO PETER

We were, fair Queen,
Two lads that thought there was no more behind
But such a day tomorrow as today,
And to be boy eternal.

Contents

Preface

The psalmist says that only those whose hands are clean and whose hearts are pure will ascend the hill of the Lord. A modern philosopher writes that the primary task of morality should be exploration of the means by which we discipline the "fat relentless ego" that is each of us. Simply put, the moral life aims at virtue. An ethic of virtue has characteristic emphases and, at least within the context of Christian theology, characteristic difficulties. In the chapters of this book, in essays that differ greatly and draw from quite different sources, I explore both the emphases and the difficulties involved in the struggle to clean our hands and purify our hearts.

An ethic which focuses on virtue rather than duty will tend to make *vision* central in the moral life. Indeed, this may be one of the great attractions of such an ethic for religious thinkers. It provides a way to break through – or bypass – debates about the relation of religion and morality. If the way we describe our dilemmas and define our obligations depends on how we see the world, if action flows from vision and vision depends upon character, then religious beliefs will inevitably be of great importance in the shaping of an ethic. Religious disciplines – like confession or prayer – may affect what we see and do by shaping the persons we are. Perhaps some truths can be seen *only* by the disciplined ego. These themes are relatively recent in academic religious ethics, but, of course, they have a long history. To explore that received tradition and some of the theological

problems it poses I have used the writings of Josef
Pieper, a wise man too much neglected among us.

An ethic which emphasizes character suggests
quite naturally an interest in character development – in
moral education. And several of these chapters, drawing on thinkers as widely separated in time as Plato and
Lawrence Kohlberg, seek to understand something
about how the "fat relentless ego" is habituated to virtue. Here also theology is relevant. If theories of moral
education must finally attempt to shape "being" through
"doing," we cannot ignore the theological challenge
which suggests that only right "being" can possibly lead
to right "doing." Our efforts at moral education are attempts to shape the ego through the discipline of
habitual behavior, but it may be that the ego needs not
just discipline but rebirth.

Indeed, before Christian ethicists latch too quickly
onto an ethic of virtue, it is important to remember that
an emphasis on character may sit uneasily with some
strands of Christian belief. No theologian has urged this
point more forcefully than Luther. The virtues are,
many have wanted to say, "good for us." A sketch of the
virtues is a picture of a fulfilled life, of the successful
realization of a self. Such an approach cannot without
difficulty be incorporated into a vision of the world
which has at its center a crucified God – which takes,
that is, not self-realization but self-sacrifice as its central theme. Furthermore, the very notion of character
seems to suggest – *has* suggested at least since
Aristotle – habitual behavior, abilities within our power,
an acquired possession. And this in turn may be difficult
to reconcile with the Christian emphasis on grace, the
sense of the sinner's constant need of forgiveness, and
the belief that we can have no claims upon the freedom
of God.

Finally, it is important to think not just about an
ethic of character but about particular virtues and vices,

about the actual traits of character which we seek to inculcate or discourage. For that reason I include chapters on the vice of curiosity and the virtue of gratitude. The obvious fact that we may not regard the former as a vice and may prefer asserting our rights rather than practicing gratitude suggests only that we still have a long way to go on the endless path toward virtue.

Most of these chapters were written with the aid of a grant from the National Endowment for the Humanities, and many of them were tried out on my colleagues in the symposium on the individual and community sponsored by the Center of Theological Inquiry at Princeton Seminary during the 1982-83 academic years. It is a pleasure to be able to acknowledge the support of the Endowment and the encouragement of my colleagues at the center.

1. Thinking about Virtue

All around us are signs, if not of a revival of interest in being virtuous, at least of new interest in a theory of the virtues. And in his brilliant if idiosyncratic book *After Virtue*,[1] Alasdair MacIntrye has suggested that this interest is doomed to failure. Doomed only for the present to be sure, but surely doomed in a society which lacks the moral consensus any theory of the virtues requires. For MacIntyre, however, this is not cause for pessimism. In fact, recognizing perhaps that the virtue of hope is meant for just such times as the one he depicts, MacIntyre hopes that out of our moral chaos and degeneration may come a new version of the virtuous life. It will come, he believes, among those who fashion a social life in which virtue can have some genuine meaning.

That this is possible, and that we may have some reason for hope, MacIntyre suggests by comparing our own moment in history to that age in Europe when the Roman Empire declined into the Dark Ages.

> A crucial turning point in that earlier history occurred when men and women of good will turned aside from the task of shoring up the Roman *imperium* and ceased to identify the continuation of civility and moral community with the maintenance of *imperium*. (p. 245)

Instead, they tried to fashion new forms of common life, forms in which the virtues could be lived, sustained, and inculcated. MacIntrye's hope is that we may find ourselves at a similar moment.

> What matters at this stage is the construction of local
> forms of community within which civility and the in-
> tellectual and moral life can be sustained through the
> new dark ages which are already upon us . . . . We are
> waiting not for a Godot, but for another – doubtless very
> different – St. Benedict. (p. 245)

Thus does the twentieth-century prophet foresee a
green twig growing from the dead stump of our present
culture.

What is interesting and striking about MacIntyre's
analysis, however, is that there is in it little hint that the
new communities and new forms of the moral life which
they sustain will be rooted in or nourished by the
religious life – the reference to St. Benedict not-
withstanding. Indeed, although MacIntyre traces the
root of our moral disorder to the loss of *both* the
teleological element in traditional morality (inherited, to
put it too simply, from Aristotle) and the deontological
element (inherited, to put it too simply, from Christian
notions of divine law), it is significant that his attempt
at reconstructing a theory of the virtues seems to
assume that we can recapture only the Aristotelian half
of our tradition and that the Christian half is gone
forever.

We may compare this with an observation from
Josef Pieper's *Scholasticism*.[2] Pieper notes that it is impossible to give any specific date for the beginning of
the medieval period. But he suggests that we consider
the "special symbolic significance" of the year 529 A.D.
In that year the Platonic Academy, which had existed in
Athens for nine hundred years, was closed by the Christian emperor Justinian. And in that same year, as pagan
philosophy was brought to a kind of symbolic close, St.
Benedict founded Monte Cassino. "Here, then, we find
something very much like a visible boundary where a dy-

ing and a newborn age touch one another" (p.17). Pieper suggests that Boethius also stands at this point of turning. He perhaps believed that his philosophic work could be carried on in the court of the German ruler Theodoric – and his death was proof that he was mistaken. Boethius' younger contemporary Cassiodorus evidently realized this, for he left his position among the officialdom of Theodoric's court and founded a monastery. And, Pieper notes, "for almost a thousand years to come Boethius remained the last 'layman' in the history of European philosophy" (p. 41).

Thus, Pieper points to the same moment in history which MacIntyre notes. Pieper also suggests that we consider as a symbol for the end of the medieval period the day when William of Ockham reversed the direction of Cassiodorus' turn and fled from the cloister to the German imperial court. From that time philosophy once again took up its residence in the world (p. 155). But then, remembering what this has meant for our time, Pieper sounds a note which is, as I have said, strikingly absent from MacIntyre's hope. What has happened since William of Ockham's turn toward the world, since philosophy lost the churchly context for its work?

> Do we not find ourselves somewhat caught in the modern world of work – faced with the increasing politicalization of the academic realm and the ominous shrinking of inner and outer opportunities for public discourse, and especially for genuine debate? Where shall we seek the "free area" in which alone *theoria* can thrive . . . ? We begin to understand that Plato's Academy had been a *thiasos*, a religious association assembling for regular sacrificial worship. Does this have any bearing on our time? (p. 155)

We may hope that it does – and that it can have some effect on what we think about virtue.

The Return of Virtue

Our initial problem, however, may simply be with the word 'virtue'. Who today wishes to be virtuous? Who today even uses the word? If we talk of this topic at all, we are more likely to speak of character than virtue; for 'character' seems to suggest those cardinal virtues of our time, sincerity and authenticity – in short, being true to oneself. 'Virtue', by contrast, may still carry a little of its older meaning: standards by which to measure and evaluate the self we are.

In reality, of course, the word 'virtue' may not suggest such standards either, because it may suggest little or nothing to most of our contemporaries. There are still some of us alive who can enjoy singing the words of the hymn: "cry out dominions, princedoms, powers / *virtues*, archangels, angels' choirs." But it is to be doubted whether we often think of virtue as a power inherent in a natural or supernatural being, whether we proceed from that thought to one of an embodiment of such power, and from thence to a virtue as one of the ranks of celestial beings – though the *Oxford English Dictionary* suggests such a progression of thought. Even in this liberated age the word 'virtue' probably suggests for us more often another of the meanings the dictionary gives: "chastity, sexual purity, esp. of women." And when we consider that meaning of the word in light of the question "Who today wishes to be virtuous?" we can only respond with another question from another well-known hymn: "Oh where are ye, ye virgins wise?"

Nevertheless, whatever difficulties the word may present, it is a fact that many students of ethics – both philosophical and theological – are returning today to something which may be called an ethic of virtue. This return suggests a widespread dissatisfaction with an understanding of the moral life which focuses primarily on duties, obligations, troubling moral dilemmas, and borderline cases. Such cases are interesting, and certainly important when they arise, but we must admit that many of us go through long stretches of life in which we do not have to decide whether to frame one innocent man in order to save five, whether to lie to the secret police in order to hide someone, whether to approve aborting the ninth, possibly retarded, child of a woman whose husband has deserted her, and so forth. An ethic of virtue seeks to focus not only on such moments of great anxiety and uncertainty in life but also on the continuities, the habits of behavior which make us the persons we are. Not whether we should frame one innocent man to save five – but on the virtue of justice, with its steady, habitual determination to make space in life for the needs and claims of others. Not whether to lie to the secret police – but on that steady regard for others which uses language truthfully and thereby makes a common life possible. Not whether abortion is permissible in an extreme case – but on the ancient question Socrates raised, whether it is better to suffer wrong than to do it. An ethic of virtue turns away not only from an overemphasis on borderline cases but also from the concept of duty as the central moral concept. *Being* not *doing* takes center stage; for what we ought to do may depend on the sort of person we are. What duties we perceive may depend upon what virtues shape our vision of the world.

If the turn toward an ethic of virtue is motivated in part by a desire to focus attention on continuities in the development of character rather than primarily on difficult and agonizing borderline cases, we might imagine that this is a turn toward simplicity and away from complex, complicated ethical systems. In some ways, however, the opposite may be the case. We cannot really talk very long about virtue without speaking of virtues – of particular moral excellences which go by various names. Indeed, enshrined in Western moral tradition at least

from the time of Plato's *Republic* are the names of four
cardinal virtues – prudence (practical wisdom), justice,
courage, and temperance. These are the cardinal virtues
because they form the hinge or axis (*cardo*) on which the
moral life turns. To this tradition of four cardinal virtues Christian thought added the triumvirate of theological virtues – faith, hope, and love. What we begin to
have, then, is a complicated ethic capable of distinguishing many different traits of character and habits of behavior. This is not an ethic which can talk only of obligation, or only of authenticity, or only of love. It is an ethic
which will permit us more by way of moral evaluation
than judgments of right and wrong. Thus, even if on
some occasion we cannot condemn a particular act as
wrong, our powers of moral evaluation are not paralyzed. What we do not condemn as wrong we may de-
plore as, for example, intemperate. Some theorists, as
we will see, still wish to argue a sense in which all the
virtues are one – that, for example, all might finally be
forms of love. But this is not a claim that henceforth we
should speak only of love, nor a claim that we should
deprive ourselves of the nuance and shades of meaning
which an ethic of virtue provides.

The Meaning of Virtue

In thinking about virtue it is useful to begin with a
definition, and Josef Pieper's is a good place to start. In
his Preface to *The Four Cardinal Virtues* Pieper suggests that the virtues are those excellences which enable
a human being "to attain the furthest potentialities of
his nature."[3] This suggests at the outset that no list of
virtues can be made from neutral ground, that any list
will reflect beliefs about human nature and its possibilities.

Even more important perhaps is the suggestion that the virtues have to do with "the furthest potentialities" of our nature. They call attention not only to certain basic obligations which we owe each other; they call us out on an endless quest toward the perfection of our being. Aristotle – to whose theory of the virtues everyone sooner or later returns – writes that moral activity is a kind of doing rather than making. When we shape and mold character we are not creating an artifact which is fixed forever. There can be no preconceived blueprint of what a person ought to be, no science of morals. To attempt virtue is to set out on a quest which lasts as long as life does.

These general reflections, suggestive as they may be, provide no detailed description of what we mean by a virtue. To attempt some of that detail we can consider in turn three possiblities which are often suggested – that virtues are dispositions to act in certain ways, that they are skills, and that they are traits of character.

The first possibility – often characterized in terms of the relation between being and doing – is that the virtues should be analyzed as dispositions to act in certain ways. Obviously, of course, some kinds of activity seem incompatible with certain virtues. We will be inclined to doubt whether one who gains all he can but does not (as Wesley advised) give all he can but simply reinvests it for his own purposes can really be moved by the virtue of justice (much less generosity or love). We may doubt whether someone who turns and runs from danger can really be moved by the virtue of courage. We may doubt – but we cannot be certain. The man who runs from danger may in fact be courageous. And although this will not lead us to characterize running from danger as an "act of courage," it is still an act that might be done by a courageous man.[4] Similarly, the woman who gains all she can may simply have taken the lessons of supply-side economics to heart; she may truly believe that she serves the just interests of her neighbors when she invests and reinvests her capital. If the virtues offer no preconceived blueprint for human life, we should expect such possibilities. We should anticipate some connection between the virtues and external categories of acts but never a perfect or tight fit. *"The path of virtue is never laid out in advance."*[5]

This means that we must disagree with a claim like William Frankena's that "one cannot conceive of traits of character except as dispositions and tendencies to act in certain ways in certain circumstances."[6] Virtuous states do not correspond perfectly with a disposition to any set of acts and, in addition, the virtuous act may be achieved without the virtue. I may face danger without fleeing, but this does not make me courageous. It may, as Hobbes knew, only show that I am still more fearful of some other danger.

If virtues are not simply dispositions to act in certain ways, we may come closer to the mark if we understand them as skills. (And in so doing we follow Aristotle.) Certainly if a skill is simply the ability to do a certain sort of act proficiently, we may not wish to call the virtues skills, for to associate them so intimately with specific activities may miss the open texture of the virtues which we have already noted. At the very least, we cannot say that the virtues are skills in any particular activity. As G. H. von Wright has noted, "being courageous" does not name a particular activity. As an answer to the question "What are you doing?" it will not suffice to reply: "I am being courageous; this is very dangerous."[7]

One way to make clearer what is at stake here is to note that the virtues are not simply techniques. And, as long as we keep this in mind, it may help to think of them as skills – but skills which suit us for life generally, not just for some particular activity. The virtues are skills which are learned, not techniques which are taught. It is the difference between learning to cook and following the directions in a cook book, between learning to drive a car and passing one's written test after studying the manual, between living as a Christian and studying the catechism.[8] A skilled craftsman (just as rare these days as a virtuous person) has not just mastered a technique; he has acquired a skill which permits him to respond creatively to new situations or unanticipated difficulties.[9] His skill is not usually taught in a classroom but is learned by apprenticeship.

We come closer to describing virtues properly, then, if we consider them skills – but skills which fit us for life in general. Even this is not a fully adequate account. The difficulties in being virtuous are often not due to difficulties in the virtuous actions themselves (as are the difficulties facing a skilled craftsman) but are, instead, due to our own "contrary inclinations."[10] Philippa Foot has made this point by noting that, while skills are only capacities, virtues actually engage the will. If I deliberately miss a baseball pitched to me, it does not show that I lack the skill to hit it. But if while playing baseball I deliberately treat the opposing team unjustly, this does indicate that I lack a certain virtue. If someone, seeing me miss the pitch, says I lack the skill to hit, I can respond by saying that I missed it deliberately. But if someone accuses me of unjust behavior I cannot excuse myself by saying "I did it deliberately."[11] Virtues engage the will in a way that skills do not.

Even here it is worth noting – to stick with my baseball analogy – that if I deliberately miss the pitch too often I am likely to develop some deficiencies in my swing (a hitch, moving the back foot) which will make me a less proficient hitter. Something similar is true of the virtues. Contrary inclinations, vice, may be gradually learned. To make a moral mistake too often, even to do it deliberately as one might miss a pitch, may gradually engage the will. This was Bonhoeffer's worry

when he questioned whether he and those like him could
still be of any use when Germany's crisis was past.

> We have been the silent witnesses of evil deeds.
> Many storms have gone over our heads. We have learnt
> the art of deception and of equivocal speech. Experience
> has made us suspicious of others and prevented us from
> being open and frank. Bitter conflicts have made us
> weary and even cynical. Are we still serviceable? It is
> not the genius that we shall need, not the cynic, not the
> misanthropist, not the adroit tactician, but honest,
> straightforward men. Will our spiritual resources prove
> adequate and our candour with ourselves remorseless
> enough to enable us to find our way back again to
> simplicity and straightforwardness?[12]

To lie in a good cause for the first time may not show
that we lack the virtue of truthfulness; it might make
good sense to note that we did it deliberately. But
Bonhoeffer's concern is a valid one: to do this too often
may gradually engage the will in vice, and it may be difficult to "find our way lack again to simplicity and
straightforwardness." Virtues are like skills in that they
require constant practice.[13]

Nevertheless, since virtues engage the will in a way
that skills do not, they are perhaps best thought of not
simply as skills but as traits of character. When virtues
are described in this way, we can appreciate the
significance of a point Stanley Hauerwas has made. "As
persons of character we do not confront situations as
mud puddles into which we have to step; rather the kind
of 'situations' we confront and how we understand them
are a function of the kind of people we are."[14] Given certain traits of character we may be enabled to see those
mud puddles as occasions for rejoicing and opportunities
for being rid of our shoes. Hence, the virtues do not just
equip us for certain activities, or even for life in general;
they influence how we describe the activities in which

we engage, what we think we are doing and what we think important about what we are doing. Our virtues and vices affect our reaction to the events of life, but they also determine in part the significance of those events for us. To see this is to understand why *vision* is likely to be a central theme in any ethic of virtue. Our virtues do not simply fit us for life; they help shape life. They shape not only our character but the world we see and inhabit. Roger Wertheimer once speculated that if wombs were transparent – enabling us to see fetuses developing – we might think differently about abortion.[15] Perhaps. But perhaps not. For what we saw there might be as different as our characters are different. Some might see fetuses – others, unborn children – developing. The moral virtues – those excellences which help us attain the furthest potentialities of our nature – are, then, not simply dispositions to act in certain ways. They are more like skills which suit us for life generally – and still more like traits of character which not only suit us for life but shape our vision of life, helping to determine not only who we are but what world we see.

The Need for Virtue

Why do we need these virtues? We can distinguish two general answers to this question. Some emphasize that the virtues have a kind of corrective function, helping to control and direct our emotions.[16] Others stress the fact, not necessarily incompatible with the first emphasis, that the virtues fit us to live a life characteristic of flourishing human beings.[17]

It is not, I think, sufficient to think of the virtues only in the former way – only as character traits designed to strengthen us in the face of temptation. For it would seem that the greater our virtue the less susceptible to temptation we would be – and, then, the better the person, the less virtuous he or she would be. This is, of course, an old argument: whether perfect virtue would be effortless and habitual, or always in the face of contrary inclinations.

Philippa Foot mitigates the difficulty somewhat when she suggests that "the thought that virtues are corrective does not constrain us to relate virtue to difficulty in each individual man."[18] She offers the example of someone with an opportunity to steal. If in such a situation a person is tempted, his virtue is less. But if a person is poor and this situation is therefore tempting, his virtue is greater when he does not steal.[19] This person's virtuous behavior might be habitual and effortless in such circumstances, but this does not alter the fact that for human beings in general such circumstances are tempting. Hence, a virtue like justice is needed; it plays a corrective role in directing and governing our emotions.

Perhaps the point of the virtues often lies in such direction and guidance, but not always. To take a virtue not ranked too highly these days, we may contrast chastity as *continence* with chastity as *temperance*.[20] Chastity as continence suggests "strenuous control," that directing and guiding of emotion which virtue sometimes requires. But chastity as temperance, the perfected virtue, "bears the joyous, radiant seal of ease, of effortlessness." It suggests not merely that our emotions are governed and ordered, but that we have begun to approach the furthest potentialities of our nature, that we are living life characteristic of flourishing human beings. Or, to take a different example, if the apostle is correct in believing that "love abides" even in heaven, it will not be sufficient to say with Foot that human beings need the virtue of charity simply because they are prone to self-love.[21] They need it also to flourish as human beings – for adornment, even when temptation has ceased to trouble them.

Why do we need the virtues? They are traits of character needed "for living well the sort of life that is characteristic of human beings." To say this is *almost* to return to Pieper's statement that the virtues enable a human being "to attain the furthest potentialities of his nature." These two statements *will* be the same if it turns out that a life characteristic of human beings is an endless journey toward perfection.

The Danger of Virtue

We have discussed some of the reasons ethicists are turning or returning to an ethic of virtue, and we have considered what it means to speak of moral virtues and why human beings need and value them. But we will think more clearly about virtue if we consider yet one problem. Some day, when a historian writes a history of ethics in twentieth-century America, perhaps he or she will note that the turn in ethics to a concentration upon self, development of the self's character and vision, and the turn to an emphasis upon being rather than doing were not unexpected turns in an increasingly narcissistic age. We should consider therefore the possibility that even those thinkers who have returned to notions of virtue in an attempt to escape the individualism of our times – and there are such thinkers – may be part of a larger current of history in which their turn is only a small part of an increasingly dangerous concentration upon self and self-development. Perhaps a moral notion like *duty* serves better than *virtue* to focus our attention on the needs of others.

In his essay "Utilitarianism and Moral Self-Indulgence," Bernard Williams addresses himself to one version of this problem.[22] He is concerned about circumstances in which there might be strong utilitarian reasons for doing what a person whose character was formed by certain virtues – justice, generosity, fidelity, courage – would not do. And the question is: if in such a case we refuse to do what considerations of utility call for, can we be charged with moral self-indulgence? Could someone quite properly accuse us of displaying "a possessive attitude" toward our virtue (p. 306)?

Concentration upon the virtues may tempt us to self-indulgence by leading us to what Williams calls a reflexive concern. That is, not only do I act with gratitude, but I act from a conception of myself as one who acts gratefully. "It is one thing," as Williams puts it, "for a man to act in a counter-utilitarian way out of his great love for Isolde, another for him to do so out of a concern for his image of himself as a great Tristan" (p. 312). Thus, in connection with a virtue like gratitude I may have both a first-order motivation (gratitude itself) and a second-order motivation (seeing myself as a person who acts gratefully). The first-order motivation focuses my attention on the one to whom I show my gratitude. The second-order motivation is reflexive because it subtly directs my attention and concern back to myself rather than the one to whom gratitude is given. No doubt an ethic of duties is subject to the same danger; I may act from a conception of myself as one who is dutiful. But perhaps an ethic of virtue is more beset by this danger because of its emphasis upon character and character development.

Despite these dangers, Williams points out that there are occasions on which acting from such a second-order motivation may be quite appropriate (p. 313). If I feel little gratitude toward benefactors, the best I can manage may be to act from the conception of myself as grateful. It may be a salutary moral discipline for me to ask myself, "What would I do if I acted as a grateful person would act here?" And, if Aristotle is correct in holding that we become virtuous by doing virtuous deeds, acting out of such reflexive self-concern may gradually make a better person of me. I may learn to be grateful, not just to act out of concern for my self-image as a grateful person. In this sense, hypocrisy is not always bad in the moral life. Thus, for example, C. S. Lewis tells how he came to know a young man in the army. First drawn to him by common intellectual interests, Lewis soon became impressed with what seemed the superior virtue of his new friend.

> There was no discussion between us on the point and I do not think he ever suspected the truth about me. I was at no pains to display it. If this is hypocrisy, then I must conclude that hypocrisy can do a man good. To be ashamed of what you were about to say, to pretend that something which you had meant seriously was only a joke – this is an ignoble part. But it is better than not to be ashamed at all. And the distinction between pretending you are better than you are and beginning to be better in reality is finer than moral sleuthhounds conceive.[23]

First- and second-order motivations can be distinguished in thought, but they are harder to separate in our psyches.

Even if there is something good to be said for such reflexive concern to see oneself acting as a virtuous person would act, it would be hard to deny that this reflexive concern may often divert our attention from others to self – and once our attention is diverted, our action may be as well. Alasdair MacIntyre, I noted at the outset, suggests that within the moral chaos of our culture we are waiting for a new St. Benedict. Waiting, that is, for those who will establish new forms of community within which the virtues can be inculcated, lived, and sustained. Perhaps we are. But it is worth remembering – even though MacIntyre surely is not calling for a revival of monasticism – what Beach and Niebuhr termed "The Problem of the Monastic Way."[24] For the monk, dedicated to the cultivation of virtue, "Self-conquest is always the first ethical task." The prob-

lem of the monastic way is that the task may be sub-
stituted for the goal. Beach and Niebuhr put it nicely in
an academic metaphor.

> The monastery was to be a lifelong "school of the Lord's
> service," where strict discipline and exactly prescribed
> "steps" might lead to the "commencement" of spiritual
> perfection. But in the curriculum of salvation the monk
> could easily become more concerned with his relation to
> the discipline than to the end for which the discipline
> was set, or, to speak by analogy, more concerned about
> getting grades than wisdom . . . . He was encouraged to
> try to outdo his fellow monks in humility; hence he might
> look down on those whom he had surpassed. Thus the
> deadly sin of pride, in the guise of its opposite, forever
> shadowed the monk as he struggled to achieve humility,
> a shadow inevitable in an ethics that conceives
> blessedness as something to be achieved by the self-
> conscious self.[25]

That self-consciousness about self is the fate which may
too easily await a concentration upon virtue. At the very
least we should say that in order to be saved from such
a fate an ethic of virtue will have to find its place within
some larger pattern of faith which affirms that we are
what we have received, and that the virtues are not
simply human achievements.

For who among us is really able to make some judgment upon his character as a whole, to be *self*-conscious
in the full sense? Who can say that he *possesses* virtue?
An ethic of virtue will be safe in our hands only as we
learn the lesson Robert Meagher finds in St. Augustine:
"Self-knowledge would require a moment in which the
whole of one's life would be simultaneously present and
available to sight."[26] Such a moment – an eternal moment – is never ours. Who am I? What judgment shall I
make of my character? All we can do in answer to such
questions is tell the story of our life, a narrative made

up of successive moments. But we have and can achieve
no privileged perspective upon the whole. Our alternatives therefore are two: We can simply tell our story
in all its successive moments, sincerely and authenti-
cally – content to believe that such authenticity is the
cardinal requirement of the moral life. Or we can tell our
story as Augustine did – not saying simply "such was my
life and character," but *confessing* "the faithful or
faithless character of that life" to One who sees it whole,
not just in its successive moments.[27]

An ethic of virtue is dominated by the eye, by
metaphors of sight and vision. To know what traits of
character qualify as virtues we must *see* our world and
human nature rightly. To *see* rightly, in turn, requires
that we have the virtues. Virtue enhances *vision*; vice
darkens and finally *blinds*. All this is important and
true, but it remains the case that we cannot see our
character or anyone else's whole and entire. We cannot
gain that privileged perspective from which such perfect
vision is possible. Because we cannot, we need not just
the eye but the ear. No ethic of virtue will be safe without a spirit of confession always ready to hear the divine
word which – seeing us whole – condemns even the best
of our virtues, and again – seeing us whole in Christ –
says, even with reference to much that does not get into
the self-conscious life stories we narrate, "well done."
Perhaps, then, the St. Benedict for whom we wait is not
so different from the first one.[28]

2. The Tradition of Virtue
Explorations in the Thought of Josef Pieper

If many ethicists have only recently turned or returned to examining the place of virtues in the moral life, the same cannot be said of the German Catholic philosopher Josef Pieper. The political theorist J. G. A. Pocock has recently enunciated his First Law of inter-disciplinary communication: "Nearly all methodological debate is useless, because nearly all methodological debate is reducible to the formula: You should not be doing your job; you should be doing mine."[1] Pieper seems to have realized the grim truth in Pocock's humor, for in his academic career he has simply proceeded to do what he is doing – write about the virtues, long before it became fashionable to do so.

Pieper has not, perhaps, attempted to develop what we would call a theory of the virtues; rather he has been content to transmit and revitalize a Thomist vision of the virtuous life. In the process he has written much of extraordinary interest. His book *The Four Cardinal Virtues*[2] is well known. Perhaps less well known are his books *Belief and Faith*,[3] *About Love*,[4] and *Uber die Hoffnung*[5] (unfortunately never translated into English, though some of Pieper's reflections on hope are available in *Hope and History*[6]). These books taken together constitute a discussion of the four cardinal and the three theological virtues. The style of the books, thoughtful and compressed, suggests that they are the product of careful, unhurried reflection on much that has been important in the Western moral tradition. By considering his views on some controverted topics we may, therefore, learn more about the virtues, more about a thinker too much neglected, and more of the meaning and significance of virtue in our moral tradition.

In his Preface to *The Four Cardinal Virtues* Pieper suggests a framework within which we are to understand human virtue. Virtues enable a person "to attain the furthest potentialities of his nature."[7] That is, the word 'virtue' does not just point toward some ensemble of desirable character traits; it suggests the utmost that a human being can be.[8] Because this is true, because virtue involves a quest for perfection, we are always "on the way" – never fulfilled, never completed. We are "ganz und gar dynamische Wirklichkeit" – and therefore, because we are not yet perfected, we experience the *ought* of duty in our lives.[9] The virtues picture for us what a person would be if his or her nature were fully realized. And, for Pieper at least, no such depiction can be adequate if it ignores the God-relation, if it lacks a vision of human beings as *creatures*. "To be a creature means: to be continually receiving being and essence from the divine Source and Creator, and in this respect, therefore, never to be finally completed."[10] Virtue is not finally or simply a possession; it is a quest for what can only be received.

The Unity of the Virtues

In "The Problem of Thor Bridge," one of Sir Arthur Conan Doyle's Sherlock Holmes stories, Dr. Watson provides the following description of Mr. Neil Gibson, who has come to consult with Holmes: "His tall, gaunt, craggy figure had a suggestion of hunger and rapacity.

An Abraham Lincoln keyed to base uses instead of high ones would give some idea of the man."[11] One of the interesting questions about the virtues is whether something like this is possible: a man with Lincoln's virtues, but with those virtues "keyed to base uses instead of high ones." The question is at least as old as Plato: Are the virtues one? Must a man who possesses one virtue necessarily have them all? Must a woman who lacks one really lack them all?

Clearly, some of the virtues *are* interrelated. For example, without at least some courage it may be difficult to have any other virtue; for without courage we may be unable to do what other virtues call for in difficult circumstances. Similarly, there may be a special relationship between prudence and the other virtues such that prudence is impossible without other virtues and the other virtues cannot be had apart from prudence. To that question we return later. There are also theological contexts in which one might wish to stress the unity of the virtues – to say with St. Augustine that even the great virtues of the noble Romans were ultimately "splendid vice," since they were not ordered toward the love of God.

An emphasis on the unity of the virtues comes naturally to those who believe that the moral life is harmonious, a seamless robe which must either be worn intact or not at all. For adherents of such a view there must be some single best way of life for all human beings – however general the terms may be in which we describe it. Any conflict within the moral life must result not from the absurdity or tragedy of our world but from the flaws in our character. Had Lincoln's character been keyed to those base uses rather than high ones, he could not have displayed all the virtues we ascribe to him.

Such an emphasis on the necessary unity of the virtues may seem bizarre and counterintuitive. Can we not admire the courage of the spy or soldier committed to what we think an evil cause? Are not men often temperate because they are too proud to act otherwise? Are not generosity and injustice quite compatible in certain circumstances? And, in general, do we not often develop many virtues for the sake of pursuing one great vice?

If there is good reason to speak of a multiplicity of virtues which need not be one, it is the reason given by Charles Williams in a memorable sentence: "Deep, deeper than we believe, lie the roots of sin; it is in the good that they exist; it is in the good that they thrive and send up sap and produce the black fruit of hell."[12] If we acknowledge no possibility for tension among the virtues, we may not be able to account adequately for the powerful attraction which evil often holds. Injustice recognized and affirmed as injustice will rarely tempt us. But injustice in the name of generosity – true, tender, and suffering generosity – may seduce us to vice under the guise of virtue.

There are moments when Pieper appears to adopt the view that the virtues are many and need not coexist. "We ought," he writes, "to be prepared to find that the most powerful embodiment of evil in human history, the Antichrist, might well appear in the guise of a great ascetic."[13] Perhaps, however, we must emphasize the words "in the guise of," for elsewhere Pieper suggests that the virtues are one. He notes, for instance, that courage involves more than just risking one's person. It presumes the "correct evaluation of things" which prudence gives; it presumes that the possible gain is worth the risk.[14] If this were not the case, how could we distinguish courage from foolhardiness? We are likely to agree with him here, less likely when he goes on to claim that courage is also impossible without justice. That is, a courage which is not in service of justice is "false and unreal." He cites St. Augustine: "Not the injury, but the cause makes martyrs."[15]

Does it make a difference whether the virtues are many or one? Does anything important turn on our decision about this question? If we are impressed primarily with the tragic choices often encountered in the moral life, we are likely to believe that the many virtues are *not* one – that someone may well be courageous in an unjust cause, temperate (even a great ascetic) while torturing the innocent, and so forth. If, on the other hand, we are impressed primarily with the fact that judgments of character are made, finally, not upon isolated virtues or vices but upon persons, we are likely to believe that the many virtues are one – that any defect in virtue must to some extent permeate and corrupt the entire self, leaving only seeming virtues or splendid vices. We are often moved by those who stress the tragic features of moral choice, but we pay a price for savoring the tragic too much. We compartmentalize human character, we settle for isolated virtues, and we may lose the sense that to seek virtue is to set out on an endless quest requiring not just certain character traits but a transformation of the self.

Whatever we may say about a general thesis concerning the unity of the virtues, it is instructive to turn to the particular question of the relation between prudence and other virtues. Pieper suggests a very intimate bond between prudence – the ability to see what is really there – and the other cardinal virtues. Knowledge and virtue are one. In *The Silence of Saint Thomas* Pieper tells the old story of how Thomas, desiring to become a Dominican, was waylaid and held captive by his brothers in the hope that he could be persuaded to change his mind. The story is that his brothers engaged a courtesan to tempt him but that Thomas drove her from his room – and was thereafter miraculously protected against any temptation to unchastity. A quaint story, we are likely to think. But Pieper discerns a deeper message.

Since we nowadays think that all a man needs for acquisition of truth is to exert his brain more or less vigorously, and since we consider an *ascetic* approach to knowledge hardly sensible, we have lost the awareness of the close bond that links the knowing of truth to the condition of purity. Thomas says that unchastity's first-born daughter is blindness of the spirit. Only he who wants nothing for himself, who is not subjectively "interested," can know the truth. On the other hand, an impure, selfishly corrupted will-to-pleasure destroys both resoluteness of spirit and the ability of the psyche to listen in silent attention to the language of reality.[16]

The suggestion is that in order to know the truth one must be a person of a certain sort. And, indeed, this is a theme of central importance for the Aristotelian tradition in ethics, the theme that ethics can be taught only to those already possessed of good moral habits.

The implications for ethics are staggering. If the history of twentieth-century ethics is largely a history of metaethical disputes, it is fair to say that in the most elementary sense these disputes have been sparked by the seeming endlessness and futility of moral argument. This sense of futility has led many to conclude that one's choice of moral principles and adoption of habits of behavior must be simply that: a choice or stance, a decision which can make no claim to be knowledge of truth. The assumption, of course, is that all parties to the dispute are entitled to equal hearing, that as Alasdair MacIntyre has put it, the moral agent (whose views must be counted in such disputes) "is anyone and everyone not actually mentally defective."[17] Pieper, by contrast, adheres to an older view which held that our intellects are not to be creative but to be conformed to the truth of things – and that such conformity is increasingly possible only as we grow in virtue. Iris Murdoch has put the point well in a passage we will more than once have occasion to cite.

> By opening our eyes we do not necessarily see what confronts us. We are anxiety-ridden animals. Our minds are continually active, fabricating an anxious, usually self-preoccupied, often falsifying *veil* which partially conceals the world. . . . And if quality of consciousness matters, then anything which alters consciousness in the direction of unselfishness, objectivity and realism is to be connected with virtue.[18]

Calling to mind the story of St. Thomas, we might consider whether chastity is one of those things which "alters consciousness in the direction of unselfishness, objectivity and realism" – and therefore a necessary condition for ethical insight. It is only one example among many which might be given – perhaps not even the best example – but it suggests what a misleading turn ethics might have taken in our century, and it raises questions about our ability really to teach ethics in the ordinary academic context.

The suggestion that one must be virtuous in order to be prudent, that we cannot achieve moral knowledge and *do* the right act without first *being* to some extent virtuous, is not made in order to cut off discussion, nor is the claim made in an arrogant or rationalist spirit. It amounts only to the observation that, as John Finnis has written, "the fact that there is a controversy is not an argument against one side in that controversy."[19] Perhaps only one party in the discussion is really in a position to know the truth; perhaps none is. That there is such truth to be known Pieper derives from an understanding of the world as *created*. Things can be known because they are creatively and determinately thought by God, and prudence is the virtue which is open to that objective reality. That this is no arrogant, rationalist claim follows equally from the fact of *crea-*

tion. For though our world is knowable (because created), it is also unfathomable (because created). The relation between reality and the creative thought of God is beyond our comprehension; the same light which enlightens our intellects is too bright to be looked at directly.

> Because things come forth from the eye of God, they partake wholly of the nature of the Logos, that is, they are lucid and limpid to their very depths. It is their origin in the Logos which makes them knowable to men. But because of this very origin in the Logos, they mirror an *infinite* light and can therefore not be wholly comprehended. It is not darkness or chaos which makes them unfathomable. If a man, therefore, in his philosophical inquiry, gropes after the essence of things, he finds himself, by the very act of approaching his object, in an unfathomable abyss, but it is an abyss of *light*.[20]

This means – to note the relevance of another virtue – that hope is "the condition of man's existence as a knowing subject."[21] The quest for knowledge, also for knowledge of value and virtue, lasts as long as life.

One aspect of the relationship between prudence and the other virtues may be captured, therefore, by saying that without other virtues like justice, temperance, and courage no true prudence is possible. If prudence requires that our action be in accord with the truth of things, this requires that "the egocentric 'interests' of man be silenced in order that he may perceive the truth of real things, and so that reality itself may guide him to the proper means for realizing his goal."[22] We must be just enough to see the proper claims of others, temperate enough that our vision is not clouded by pleasures of the moment, brave enough to adhere to what we see even when it does not work to our benefit. Without the other virtues, moral knowledge, the insight into proper ends and means of action which prudence provides, cannot be had. This is a view which makes place for both freedom and reason within the moral life. Reason – because the moral truth we discern is determined by reality itself in all its complexity, not produced by our decisions of principle. Freedom – because the very ability to see our world rightly and understand what is required of us depends upon our character and, hence, our own self-determination.

This is *one* of the ways in which prudence and the other virtues could be said to be one – without the others, no prudence. But Pieper also says, following St. Thomas, that prudence is the preeminent virtue and that all virtue is necessarily prudent.[23] Without prudence, no other virtues. If when we survey the world our own needs and claims always appear foremost, we are not permitting "the truth of real things to have its way" and we cannot be just.[24] We will know what justice requires, what courage calls for, what moderation really means in different circumstances only if we are open to all values and claims of our world, only if we see the world as it really is. In this sense no virtue is possible without prudence.

If we consider both ways in which prudence and the other virtues are interrelated, we encounter an apparent anomaly. "Only the prudent man . . . can be just, brave, and temperate; yet he who is not already just, brave, and temperate cannot be prudent."[25] What we meet here is the fundamental paradox of all moral education. One must do what prudence requires in order to be virtuous. But one must be virtuous in order to do what prudence requires. Put more simply: doing what is right requires being good, but we can become good only by doing what is right. Pieper does not write treatises in moral education and does not, therefore, directly address this paradox. Rather, his discussion leaves us to wrestle with the problem: how to hand on moral knowledge in a society which often fails to inculcate the doing of what is right. We tend to assume that moral knowledge and virtuous activity are separable. Pieper suggests that they are not as easily divided as we imagine, and he thereby sets for us the terms of an important problem for ethical reflection.[26]

Natural and Christian Virtue

Consider the first two paragraphs of a prayer in John Baillie's *A Diary of Private Prayer*:

O omnipresent One, beneath whose all-seeing eye our mortal lives are passed, grant that in all my deeds and purposes to-day I may behave with true courtesy and honour. Let me be just and true in all my dealings. Let no mean or low thought have a moment's place in my mind. Let my motives be transparent to all. Let my word be my bond. Let me take no unchivalrous advantage of anybody. Let me be generous in my judgment of others. Let me be disinterested in my opinions. Let me be loyal to my friends and magnanimous to my opponents. Let me face adversity with courage. Let me not ask or expect too much for myself.

Yet, O Lord God, let me not rest content with such an ideal of manhood as men have known apart from Christ. Rather let such a mind be in me as was in Him. Let me not rest till I come to the stature of His own fullness. Let me listen to Christ's question: *What do ye more than others?* And so may the threefold Christian graces of faith, hope, and love be more and more formed within me, until all my walk and conversation be such as becometh the gospel of Christ.[27]

Clearly, this is a prayer several notches above the more recent "Are You Walking With Me, God?" *genre*, and it is tempting to suggest that we must take seriously the theological views of anyone who can treat the English language with such loving attention. Nevertheless, the prayer also raises – and suggests an answer to – an important problem for the Christian life. It suggests that the natural virtues – courtesy, justice, truthfulness, loyalty, courage – are whole and intact, in no special need of grace before they can come to fruition in a person's life. And the prayer suggests as well that the relation between these natural virtues and the specifically grace-given virtues of faith, hope, and love is that the latter provide a needed supplement to the former. The "ideal of manhood . . . known apart from Christ" is not mistaken, merely insufficient. It is good as far as it goes, but the Christian should not rest content with it. At issue here is the question of the sense, if any, in which Christian ethics is different from ethics, and the Christian moral life from the moral life. Is the Christian moral life all of a piece? Or is there a great discontinuity between the sort of virtue we can achieve by human effort and the virtue which is made possible by divine grace? To this issue of continuity or discontinuity and of uniqueness within the Christian life we now turn.

John Baillie's prayer suggests one of the classic answers that can be given this question: The Christian life comes in two stages, one naturally acquired, the other grace-given. Thus there is something unique about Christian morality but nothing that is radically discontinuous with our natural morality. The theological virtues cannot be acquired apart from grace but, once acquired, they fit harmoniously with the virtues naturally acquired. Roughly speaking, this is the answer we usually associate with Thomist thought (at least, all of us do who have been instructed and marked by H. Richard Niebuhr's *Christ and Culture*). Since Josef Pieper writes as one who passes on the teaching of St. Thomas, it is the answer we might expect from him.

Pieper treats the relation between natural and theological virtues in a number of places, and we can

look at several representative discussions. His treatment of the relation between prudence and charity –
chief among the natural and theological virtues
respectively – is especially instructive.[28] Following St.
Thomas, Pieper states that charity is the form of all the
other virtues, including prudence. This means that it
helps to shape and direct prudence. If prudence is the
virtue which enables us to perceive the truth of things,
charity must shape that prudence-governed perception.
Thus, Pieper can distinguish a "natural prudence" from
a "Christian prudence," the difference being that Christian prudence is (in faith) open to reality in a more all-
inclusive sense, open even to "new and invisible
realities." Indeed, Pieper says – suggesting, if we read
carefully, that natural prudence cannot be merely insufficient but must be somehow distorted – that natural
prudence by itself may tend "to restrict the realm of
determinative factors of our actions to naturally ex-
perienceable realities." The point is made succinctly in a
sentence like the following: "The Christian can . . . appear to act contrary to natural prudence because in his
acting he must conform to realities which only faith
perceives."[29]

The whole of life, including a natural virtue like
prudence, is shaped and *re*shaped by charity. "The
divine love conferred by grace shapes from the ground
up and throughout the innermost core of the most commonplace moral action of a Christian. . . . " No doubt
this reshaping will not always be experienced as discontinuous with one's previous character, but there can be
little guarantee that it will not. And, in fact, Pieper
specifically rejects the view that the new life is always
"realizable in smooth and 'harmonious' development"
with the natural order. Most striking of all is the
possibility (which Pieper finds in St. Thomas) that Christians may in charity reach "a higher and extraordinary
prudence which holds as nought all the things of this

world." He is careful to distinguish this from a contempt which springs from human arrogance; nevertheless, we have here an example of the way in which charity may reshape a natural virtue in a strikingly ascetic direction.

There remains, to be sure, a kind of continuity between natural and Christian prudence. In each there is present "the fundamental attitude of justice toward the being of things and correspondence to reality." The difference is simply – but profoundly – that Christian prudence, informed by charity, sees deeper dimensions of reality in a way that significantly reshapes what prudence sees and requires. If we remember now our earlier discussion of the unity of the virtues, we can see that Pieper's treatment of the relation between prudence and charity speaks to this issue from a new angle. When we consider the natural virtues alone, it may be difficult to show that the virtues are one and that the presence of any requires the presence of all. But at another level this thesis now seems more convincing. The natural virtues are never alone – not if they are to be virtues. The Augustinian claim that apart from love for God even the greatest of the pagans could display only splendid vice is not far from Pieper's suggestion that natural prudence unduly restricts the realm of reality to ordinary experience and that this natural prudence must be reshaped by charity "from the ground up" – perhaps culminating even in that "higher prudence" which counts as nothing the things of this world. Nevertheless, Pieper is not willing to brand the natural prudence as vice, even splendid vice. He seeks to do justice to the experience of discontinuity within the Christian life without denying that at some fundamental level there must be continuity between natural prudence and a charity-informed Christian prudence.

Another discussion of the relation between natural and theological virtues is found in the concluding pages of Pieper's *About Love*.[30] Up to this point in the book

Pieper has said little about the specifically Christian virtue of *caritas* and has analyzed all love as including both
benevolence toward others and a desire for union. But
at the very end of this discussion he speaks suddenly of
"another special form of love that we have hitherto said
nothing about, at any rate not explicitly. . . . " Though
this love is not without its connections to the other loves
he has discussed, Pieper says that it is "something new
and fundamentally different."

In what does this special Christian love consist?
Pieper notes three features. (1) In all love the fundamental element is benevolent approval—"it's good that you
exist." This is the central theme of *About Love*. But in
the Christian virtue of love this same affirmation is
made, but from a different perspective and with a new
awareness. When in love we affirm the goodness of
some thing or person we become aware "of our actually
taking up and continuing that universal approval of the
Creation by which all that has been created is 'loved by
God' and is therefore good." We ally ourselves with the
Creator's affirmation of his creation. This is part of
what the virtue of Christian love involves. The result of
seeing our love from this new perspective is that both
our love and the one loved are changed. Our love
receives "a wholly new and literally absolute confirma-
tion," since it is joined with God's own love. And the one
we love, though "still someone personally and specially
intended for us, would at the same time suddenly appear
as one point of light in an infinite mesh of light." That
would seem to mean that as our act of loving is joined
with God's, we would love particular people with a love
free of exclusivity. (2) Not only is our affirmation of
others made from a new perspective, it is also made
with a "more intensive force of approval." It is possible
now to "turn to another person in a way that otherwise . . . [we] would be utterly incapable of doing." Only
of this love is it true in the fullest sense to say that it

does not let itself be provoked and that it spends itself in forlorn causes. (3) Finally, to love another from this new perspective and with this more intensive force of approval means ultimately "to love another as the possible companion of future beatitude." And, Pieper suggests, to see others in this way, to see that no one is ordinary since all may share in future beatitude, would have a profound effect on our behavior.

In these ways the Christian virtue of love is unique and goes beyond our natural loves. How shall we think of the relation between natural love and Christian love? Does *caritas* provide only a needed supplement to the other loves? Or are the two not harmonious and supplementary but discontinuous, quite different loves with little to bridge the gap between them? Here again we find the same ambiguity that was present in Pieper's discussion of the relation between natural and Christian prudence.

On the one hand, the Christian virtue of love *presupposes* the love that is ours by nature – and presupposes that this love is relatively intact. Pieper explicitly states that *caritas* "does not invalidate any of the love and affirmation which we are able to feel on our own." Rather, it takes up our own natural will to love, a will "kindled at the Creation," and exalts it to participate in the Creator's own love. In so doing, of course, *caritas* necessarily presupposes that natural love.

On the other hand, Pieper notes that the tradition has spoken not only of the *presupposing* of our natural virtue but also the *perfecting* of it. The mystery hidden in the word 'perfecting' cannot be adequately described.

> This is one of those concepts which probably can never be known and defined before it is experienced. It is simply in the nature of the thing that the apprentice can have no specific idea of what the perfection of mastery looks like from inside, and all that is going to demand of

him. Perfection always includes transformation. And transformation necessarily means parting from what must be overcome and abandoned precisely for the sake of preserving identity in change.

How different this seems from the language of presupposing! Now Pieper can even say that "the act of *caritas* is not simply a further step on the road of *eros*." The "transformation" which our natural loves must undergo "perhaps resembles passing through something akin to dying." And Pieper concludes – hauntingly – by reminding us that *caritas* has been pictured by Christians as a consuming fire and that it is therefore "much more than an innocuous piety when Christendom prays, 'Kindle in us the fire of Thy love.'"

As a third and somewhat different example we can consider the brief chapter titled "Vital, Moral, Mystic Fortitude."[31] Here the sense of harmony between natural and theological virtues is far greater than in our two previous examples, and Pieper speaks explicitly of "the continuity in the unfolding of the supernatural life." Although three levels of fortitude are distinguished – the pre-moral order of mental health, the moral order of the natural virtue, and the "supermoral" order of the theological virtue – they "can be clearly separated only in the human mind." The willingness to let go of self-concern which is a prerequisite for mental health is the foundation of both moral and theological fortitude. If we are governed by "the tense, egocentric hold of a timorous anxiety," we will be incapable of many a venture which moral and spiritual life may require. In this sense, therefore, mystic fortitude "crowns" both vital and moral fortitude. But it also pervades the lower levels in such a way that a cure for overanxiety may require the conversion of the whole person, and the moral fortitude which is willing to risk injury or death may need the hope which only grace can provide. The highest does not stand without presupposing the lowest, and the lowest is not left behind but is taken up into the highest. At each of these levels fortitude realizes "the same essential image: a willingness to accept insecurity."

In this instance, therefore, we sense little discontinuity between the natural and the theological virtue *until* we remember Pieper's claim elsewhere that true fortitude is dependent upon both prudence and justice. Prudence discerns the good; justice carries out what prudence discerns; fortitude (and temperance) strengthen us so that we do not fail to do what prudence and justice require.[32] Thus, Pieper says that "only he who is just and prudent can also be brave; to be really brave is quite impossible without at the same time being prudent and just also."[33] When we recall that natural prudence can itself be distorted and must be transformed by the greater openness of Christian prudence, we may wonder whether what passes for fortitude – and by ordinary standards *is* fortitude – will prove to be quite so continuous with the fortitude given as a supernatural gift.

We have before us now three examples of Pieper's treatment of the relation between the natural and the theological virtues, and we can perhaps generalize a bit. It is clear that the meaning of a virtue does not change at the two levels. Prudence remains a fundamental openness to the truth of things. Love is always essentially the affirmation, "it's good that you exist." Fortitude is always a willingness to accept insecurity. This suggests an essential continuity between the two levels. We may distinguish them conceptually, but in every case I think Pieper would say what he says of the levels of fortitude: that although we may separate them in thought, "in the reality of human existance they interlock."[34] The reality toward which we creatures are open is, whether we know it or not, directed toward God. Therefore, whatever is true and good in our virtue cannot be invalidated or left behind in the life which grace bestows. From this point of view the natural virtues do not so much need to be redirected as they need to be shown the goal toward which they are already directed, a goal which will crown and complete their own natural tendencies. This is the language of continuity.

The theological question to address to this language is, of course, whether it can do sufficient justice to the disorder which sin brings to the natural virtues and to the fundamental inclinations upon which those virtues are grounded. For the more we emphasize the disordering effects of sin, the more we speak the language of discontinuity. This emphasis may, in turn, lead one to suggest that the natural virtues are in need not just of completion but of redirection – and may look quite different when this takes place. At least in his discussions of prudence and love we have seen Pieper acknowledge this, but he does so while still attempting to assert the essential continuity of the entire moral life. The perfection of the natural virtues – a perfection which itself demonstrates the continuity of the virtues, since the natural virtues are perfected, not destroyed – includes transformation, and no one can say in advance of the experience what such transformation may involve. Hence, though the several levels of virtue form a continuous way, we may *experience* seemingly unbridgeable chasms along this way. We may experience a discontinuity so severe that it can even – as Pieper says in his discussion of love – seem akin to dying.

We can understand why Pieper may wish to have it both ways – experiencing discontinuity but affirming continuity. The end of the moral life is, after all, the life of *caritas*, the love of God, which makes possible a sharing in God's affirmation of his creation. And among the things which we must approve and affirm when we share in the divine approval of creation are the natural virtues, even our own. Whether the truth of this

retrospective glance from the end of the way can be
easily balanced with the experiential truth known along
the way is *the* question, and our evaluation of Pieper's
ethic of the virtues must partially depend upon how well
he has managed to make a persuasive case for both continuity and discontinuity between the virtues we
naturally acquire and the special virtues of the Christian
life.

Virtues as Possessions

"Acquiring an excellence, be it a skill or a virtue, is
not only acquiring a capacity or tendency to act in a certain way; it is also a matter of acquiring merit."[35] These
words suggest a difficulty for anyone wishing to write
about the virtues within a framework of Christian belief.
Concentration upon the gradual development of one's
character and an effort to cultivate the virtues within
one's life may, from a Christian perspective, appear
suspect. The entire effort may seem too self-centered, a
failure to focus one's attention upon God and the
neighbor. And the very fact that virtues are habits of
behavior engrained in one's character may suggest that
they become our possession and that the moral life is not
continually in need of grace.

Pieper does not directly address the problem which
the habitual character of virtuous action raises, but
some of his remarks are useful in considering what may
be at stake here. It is true, of course, that it would make
little sense to speak of a person having certain traits of
character if this gave us no clues as to how we might expect him to behave. Talk about character suggests a certain continuity of the self and expected patterns of
behavior. But it remains true that the virtues cannot be
analyzed simply as dispositions to act in certain ways.

This comes out clearly in Pieper's discussion of prudence as a perfection of the ability to *do* rather than the ability to *make*. If our deeds help shape our character, as Pieper certainly believes, it is also true that this character is not just a thing which is made. It is a continual doing. "The human self, which grows toward perfection by accomplishing the good, is a 'work' that surpasses all preconceived blueprints based upon man's calculations."[36]

This point of view underlies Pieper's criticism of over-reliance on casuistry within morality. When casuistry becomes the attempt to fashion a science of human behavior, an attempt to lay the path of virtue in advance, it takes a mistaken turn. Such casuistry may easily fall prey to "that persistent human desire to achieve security."[37] To picture a capacity to act virtuously as safely within one's possession is to misunderstand the meaning of virtue as a continual doing. This does not mean that the virtuous man or woman does not, in fact, have the capacity to act rightly – nor that we could not rely on them to do so. But it does mean that the pattern of their activity cannot be laid out in advance. The prudent and just act must be continually sought.

Of course, some people – those who really are prudent and just – will find the right act regularly, while others will not. Does not this indicate that they have acquired virtuous habits of behavior, that virtue is their possession? To this question Pieper offers, I think, two sorts of answers. The first is a qualified affirmative. We may compare his comment when discussing how happiness can be a gift if it consists in an activity (which must, of course, be *our* activity). He cites the remark made centuries ago by a commentator on the *Summa*, which remark is, he writes, "as perspicacious as it is simple: If sight were given to a blind man, he would never-

theless see with his own sense of sight."[38] That is, even
when our virtues are presupposed and understood as
ours, they remain a gift.

The other response Pieper might make to criticism
that virtue becomes a possession is to point to the virtue
of *hope*. In this life each person is a *viator*, always on the
way. Our existence is therefore characterized by a "noch
nicht"–not yet.[39] This is why the path toward virtue
must be a never ending quest, not a possession. As trav-
elers toward a fulfillment not yet given we must find
some way to come to terms with this sense that we are
"on the way." Two false answers to this experience are
often given: We may *doubt* that any fulfillment is possible; or we may seek a calm *certainty of possession*, an
assurance that we have reached the goal.[40]

These are false answers which may tempt us. The
proper response to the experience of being on the way
is, instead, the virtue of hope. If hope is one of the chief
virtues of the Christian life, how can we take refuge in
a belief that we already possess virtue? It is interesting
to note that in *Uber die Hoffnung*, an early work, Pieper
sees both Pelagianism and the Reformation *sola gratia*
as forms of presumption. Trust in "grace alone" is
presumptuous, for it suggests a certainty not only that
redemption has been achieved in Christ but that this
redemption will surely be efficacious for me – which certainty destroys the sense of "being on the way."[41] This
suggestion bears some resemblance to Protestant
criticisms of "cheap grace," but we may doubt whether
it is an adequate understanding of the Reformation *sola
gratia*. It fails, for example, to capture Luther's sense of
the continual need to hear again the gracious promise of
God – a need grounded in the "noch nicht" character of
our present existence. But the Reformers would not, I
think, disagree with Pieper's suggestion that the virtue
of hope is needed precisely because we sojourners hear
both the righteous demands of God *and* his promised

mercy. We fall into the hopelessness of doubt if we hear only the demands; into the hopelessness of presumption if we hear the promise without the demand and regard it no longer as promise but present possession.[42] In short, though virtuous action is certainly habitual to some degree, we regard it as our possession only at our peril. To think of virtue in that way is already to lose the virtue of hope.

Hence, within Pieper's understanding of the virtues there are ways to guard against the dangers to which the notion of character—with its emphasis upon stability and reliability—may lead. What about the danger of self-centeredness? Does not the very language of virtue suggest too much concentration upon self, too intense a devotion to self-cultivation? There is reason for concern here, especially when we remember that the revival within ethics of interest in the virtues has largely coincided with countless different versions of self-fulfillment and "developing one's potential" within our culture.

A good place to join the discussion is with Pieper's treatment of "Selfless Self-Preservation" which the virtue of temperance fosters.[43] First, we note that temperance is not meant to stand in isolation from the other three cardinal virtues of prudence, justice, and fortitude. In particular, prudence looks to the truth of things (to the whole of reality) and justice toward the needs and claims of fellow human beings. Only prudence and justice "do the good"; courage and temperance create the basis for this realization of the good.[44] Hence, it is correct to say that temperance turns in and focuses upon the self. "The purpose and goal of *temperantia* is man's inner order. . . ."[45] But this turn inward is only one part of the agent's being and doing, and it should not be considered in isolation. The point and purpose of temperance is that it helps us to do the good—to act prudently and justly. The self-concern which temperance seeks is

not finally in service of the self. It is in service of virtuous treatment of others. And hence, the self-preservation which temperance fosters should be selfless rather
than selfish.

Pieper also suggests that a selfless temperance is
possible only when we love God more than ourselves. It
is, he believes, simple truth that "to love God more than
himself is in accordance with the natural being of
man. . . .Consequently, the offense against the love of
God derives its self-destructive sharpness from the fact
that it is likewise in conflict with the nature and natural
will of man himself."[46] A temperance solely in service of
the self turns out to be *self*-destructive. The answer to
the danger of self-centeredness in the virtuous life
seems to be, then, that (1) we recognize the futility of
concern solely for self; and (2) our attempts to cultivate
the virtues in our life must always be ordered not merely
toward self-cultivation but toward the virtues-as-aid-to-
prudent-and-just-activity.

The Reward of Virtue

William Frankena has noted that there is a difference between saying of someone (1) "he *had* a good
life," and (2) "he *led* a good life."[47] Indeed, it is even
possible that some of those whom we would with the
least hesitation describe as having *led* a good life might
not, by many of our usual standards, be thought to have
had a good life. The morally good and the pleasant do
not always coincide; what "tastes good" does not always
nourish.[48] To note this distinction is almost inevitably to
ask whether one who *leads* a good life should also *have*
a good life, whether virtue does or ought to have any
reward.

It is fairly obvious that virtuous behavior is useful
and beneficial for societies. It is hard to imagine a society surviving if, for example, its members never display

the virtue of courage. At the same time, the brave deed which benefits society may not benefit (in the ordinary sense) the brave man or woman who enacts it. We might respond by noting that even at the individual level almost any fulfillment requires a certain kind of self-sacrifice or self-limitation. Donald Evans notes that a miserly man

> is like a person who holds on to the air inside his lungs, refusing to exhale it lest no more be available. This prevents him from taking in any fresh air as it does become available. . . .It is a vicious circle: he refuses to give, so he cannot receive, he refuses to receive, so he cannot give.[49]

There is, of course, a kind of homely truth here, but when the sacrifice is relatively great (say, of one's life) it is harder to see where the concomitant fulfillment lies.

The difficulty, as it relates to a theory of the virtues, can be stated fairly simply. The point of the virtues must be something like the description Pieper gives: to help human beings attain the furthest potentialities of their nature. Yet, if the point of being virtuous is simply that it is good for us, that it will benefit us, we seem to have lost an important dimension (to some, *the* crucial dimension) of morality; namely, that its requirements are unconditional, that they bind us even if the price of doing what morality requires is self-sacrifice. Hence, a theory of the virtues, by accenting self-fulfillment, is always in danger of missing the place of sacrifice in human life. Or, to put it rather more dramatically: "Any account of morality which does not allow for the fact that my death may be required of me at any moment is thereby an inadequate account."[50]

If virtue fulfills, how could morality require self-sacrifice? If morality may require of us a seemingly ultimate sacrifice, what's the good of it? One way to try to break free of this dilemma is to suggest that virtue is its own reward. Morality is neither unconditional and pointless demand, nor is it important simply because it will benefit us in an external way. Rather, to lead a good life *is* to have a good life, even if one should end on a cross. The good will of the virtuous person is the only thing really worth having and the one thing we cannot lose against our will. Though few are stoic enough really to follow this way thoroughly, it has a nobility which is not without its attractions. These attractions Josef Pieper recognizes and grants while yet rejecting the view that virtue is its own reward. It may be true that the virtuous deed is accompanied by a satisfaction more significant for human life than any of the usual external rewards, but to settle for this is to ask less of life than we who know ourselves as *creatures* should. Virtue does bring with it a kind of happiness, but no one can live by this happiness alone.

> Does not the moral act truly confer a satisfaction which makes for deeper happiness than any gift that one man can transmit to another? No one denies this. But what the Western theory of happiness holds is this: that man cannot live by such happiness. The deepest thirst cannot be allayed in this way; the true expectation of the human heart will not accept such a substitute. Wherever such an attitude has been attempted or asserted, it has been artificial and imposed – because it has been something against nature. The "Titan's" arrogance which wants nothing as a gift demands in reality not too much but too little. . . .[51]

Creatures are made for God; that is Pieper's fundamental premise. And they can no more live by virtue alone than by bread alone. To attempt either is to deny the fundamental truth of our being, to act "against nature." It is only one more form of self-preservation by which we seek to evade the sacrifice which virtue may require.

If virtue is not its own reward, and if morality is not a pointless demand, in what sense does virtue benefit and fulfill us? Pieper manages, I believe, to affirm that virtue brings a reward (external to itself) without losing sight of the essential place of sacrifice within human life. The key, once again, turns out to lie in the virtue of hope. Of the many things in life and of life itself Pieper says: "All these things are genuine goods, which the Christian does not toss aside and esteem but lightly – unless, indeed, to preserve higher goods the loss of which would injure more deeply the inmost core of human existence."[52]

But does this not give the game away? For does it not suggest that any sacrifice we make is always "worth making," always more than repaid since, even while making the sacrifice, we "preserve higher goods"? To this question one can only respond: yes and no. Anything can and should be sacrificed for the sake of seeing God. And there is a sense in which in so doing one always makes a good bargain; for it would be contrary to the truth of our being to sacrifice the fellowship with God for which we are made. But in reality, those who think as Pieper does are not thinking here of striking a bargain. What takes place is not at all "the result of a carefully calculated reckoning of profit and loss."[53] Not calculation but the virtue of hope is appropriate here. And if hope involves the expectation of something good for us, it also excludes confidence. In hope we know that the good for which we wait is "not at the disposal of the hoper," that we must hope for it as a gift, not as something we can acquire through wise calculation.[54] Such Christian hope, which arises precisely when all other hopes collapse, undergirds the virtues in their full development. Pieper can say, using traditional categories, that the fulfillment supernatural hope brings may not be the fulfillment of our natural hopes.[55] That is, hope bursts the boundaries of our world and does not try to define the object of hope or set any criteria for it. Not only is the day or hour of fulfillment unknown to us, but also the form in which it will occur.[56]

Such hope is a mark of the fundamental neediness

of the creature. It is the hope that we may see God, and this hope no creature ought relinquish. But only the pure in heart see God – not because only they have earned it, but because only they can really see. Only they have the true Christian prudence which makes this vision possible. Hence, the reward which is proper to virtue is something for which we may hope, but something not at our disposal. As a result, Pieper, like Alasdair MacIntyre, can turn to the image of narrative. One who hopes in this way "is truly *en route* as a *viator* up to the very moment of his death. . . ."[57] But MacIntyre seeks the meaningfulness of the virtues only within the unity of a human life as a narrative quest. In his view "the good life for man is the life spent in seeking the good life for man, and the virtues necessary for the seeking are those which will enable us to understand what more and what else the good life for man is."[58] To this Pieper might respond that, like the stoics, MacIntyre asks not too much but too little. He settles for too little. Always to hunger but never to be filled. Always thirsty but never drinking deeply from a well of "living water." This for Pieper is not enough for a creature and, therefore, not the true point of the virtues; for it offers no real place for hope. Pieper discerns a narrative which does not end with earthly life but, instead, takes its most surprising and unexpected turn precisely at what seems to be the end. And if MacIntyre would have us wait for a new St. Benedict who will teach us that the virtues can thrive only in communities of a certain kind, it may be that we can learn from Pieper not just to wait but to hope for one who would really be a new St. Benedict – that is to say, one who would envision the virtues as a way of life for creatures made to be "companions in the sharing of beatitude."[59] A longer narrative to be sure, but for Pieper a truer story.[60]

3. Teaching Ethics and Shaping Character

Learning from Plato[1]

I teach ethics. As a statement of what I do to earn a living, that is, I suppose, accurate enough. But I have come increasingly to believe that Socrates was asking the right question when he brought young Hippocrates to Protagoras. "If Hippocrates becomes a pupil of Protagoras, and goes away a better man on the very day he becomes a pupil, and makes similar progress every day as Protagoras has promised, what will he be better at, and in what respect will he make progress?" (*Protagoras*, 318d).

Socrates himself expresses doubt that virtue, moral excellence, can be taught. He notes that the Athenians, universally regarded by other Greeks as wise, always ask the opinion of experts in their public assemblies. If, for example, they need advice on some matter of shipbuilding, they ask someone with technical expertise. And if anyone who lacks such expertise rises in the assembly to offer his opinion, they "jeer at him and create an uproar." But it is different when a matter of state policy, which calls not for technical expertise but for wise judgment, is discussed. Then

> anyone can get up and give his opinion, be he carpenter, smith or cobbler, merchant or ship-owner, rich or poor, noble or low-born, and no one objects to them . . . that they are trying to give advice about something which

45

they never learnt, not ever had any instruction about. So it's clear that they don't regard that as something that can be taught. (319b-d)

On these matters, it seems, one person's opinion is as weighty as anyone else's. The Athenians do not look for technical expertise when they are deliberating about the goals they ought to pursue. Moreover, Socrates notes, even the wisest men (notably Pericles) have proved notoriously unable to transmit virtue to their sons. "And I could mention many others, good men themselves, who never made anyone better, either their own families, or anyone else" (320b). Hence, both the public practice of the Athenians and the obvious facts about their private lives awaken in one a certain suspicion which Socrates voices. "When I consider these facts, Protagoras, I don't think that excellence can be taught" (320b).

This argument in the *Protagoras* is similar to Socrates' repeated claim in the *Meno* that virtue cannot be knowledge, something teachable, since there are no teachers of it – that is to say, none who can prove successful in transmitting moral excellence. And about this argument we may wish to say with F. J. E. Woodbridge, "The argument is not impressive, but the illustrations of it are. Socrates appeals to human experience, to the widespread interest in education, to the efforts parents make in behalf of their children, to the money they spend, paying it even to gross impostors – and all without effect. . . ."[2] If correct, however, this would be a most pessimistic doctrine. We may well wonder, since we do not seem to be born virtuous, how anyone could ever attain moral excellence if virtue cannot be taught. The only answer might be that of Socrates in the *Meno* – that those who happen to have right opinions about moral matters hold them by a kind of "divine dispensation" (100a). True perhaps, but not likely to lead many people to conclude that I should continue to draw my salary. And, of course, such a conclusion might be accurate. As Woodbridge also notes, we may forget – when we are done with the verbal pyrotechnics of Socrates and Protagoras – that the dialogue began with the earnest young man Hippocrates in search of an education in morality. We have forgotten him. Socrates and Protagoras have forgotten him. He does not seem to have gotten the education he sought.[3]

We need not accept such pessimism as the final word, however. Indeed, the views Socrates expresses in the *Protagoras* and the *Meno* are by no means his or Plato's last word on the subject. In fact, by the time the *Protagoras* comes to an end, Socrates has changed his mind. Beginning with the view that virtue is not teachable, he ends in the belief that virtue is knowledge and *must* therefore be teachable. Protagoras for his part also seems to have altered his view – from his initial confident affirmation that virtue can be taught to an insistence that virtue is not knowledge (and hence, it would seem, cannot be taught). We may think also of the evidence of some of the short "Socratic" dialogues which seem to end in puzzlement. Several of these investigate the nature of a specific virtue – courage in the *Laches*, self-control in the *Charmides*, piety in the *Euthyphro*, and, we might add, justice in Book I of the *Republic*. All end in the view that we don't really know what the virtue under discussion is, though it seems to be some kind of knowledge of the good.[4]

The point of these dialogues, taken together with the *Protagoras* and *Meno*, seems not so much to answer our question as to raise it. Can virtue be taught? Is there really some knowledge to be had in matters of morality, or is one opinion just as good as another? And if there is such knowledge to be found, how is it learned and transmitted? What would it mean to teach ethics?

Teaching Virtue

Lengthy reflection is not needed to see how strikingly relevant to our own time are the questions Plato raises. It is not unusual when teaching ethics to find that a student, having written a paper carefully analyzing the arguments presented by an author about a moral problem, should then conclude (almost in these words): "Of course, this is only his opinion, one among many." This is our constant experience – that moral argument never comes to an end. Seeing this, we move quickly and easily from the observation that no moral standpoint seems universally persuasive to the conviction that no moral standpoint can claim to be true. We may still tend to use words like 'right' and 'true' about our own positions, but it is not clear how we can do so unless perhaps we have received our opinions by "divine dispensation."

This familiar fact of our moral experience has been reflected in academic ethics as well. Attempts to account for our moral experience have shifted rapidly from G. E. Moore's view that we intuit a non-natural goodness, to Sir David Ross's intuitions of *prima facie* duties, to C. L. Stevenson's claim that moral utterances are expressions of emotional attitudes, to R. M. Hare's suggestion that our moral point of view rests upon a decision of principle, to Philippa Foot's contention that morality seeks what will help us flourish as human beings. Different views – different accounts of morality. Alasdair MacIntyre seems correct, however, in suggesting that, behind the vast variety of moral points of view espoused among us, our fundamental experience is that (1) once we reach their basic premises moral arguments cannot be settled; but (2) these arguments should, nevertheless, be impersonal, not a matter merely of preference or taste.[5]

We try not to think about where this leaves us; for it may seem to leave us with no choice but battle. If it is the case not only that we disagree but that no amount of discussion can be counted on to overcome our differences, we seem left only with a war of assertion and counterassertion. Or, if the stakes are high enough, with a war not just of words. Perhaps we are often saved from that real war only by our secret belief that matters of opinion are not, finally, worth a fight.

These features of our moral experience suggest that virtue cannot be taught, that morality is not a matter of knowledge. Hence, in our classrooms we will tend to analyze moral arguments but not to evaluate basic moral stances. Some teachers prove very skilled at this – they publish articles and receive tenure. Some students are also skilled – they get an "A" in ethics. But behind all the teaching and learning is the assumption that moral points of view are not true or false, only chosen. When it comes to morality, one person's opinion is as weighty as anyone else's. One generation has no knowledge of virtue to transmit to the next. Our experience suggests that virtue cannot be taught.

When Socrates suggested as much to the men of his day, they rejected him. There were, after all, teachers of virtue all around them – the sophists. Socrates' criticism of them was simply that their skills could help their students succeed only if those students already knew what goals to pursue. But when it came time to decide about the goals, the sophists could offer only rhetorical flourishes. In our world too there is a kind of technical knowledge which can be taught. We look to doctors to tell us how to stay healthy, or what our prospects of recovering from illness are, or how severe the deformities of our unborn child may be. Such technical expertise can be taught – and there are teachers of it. But when we want to know whether staying healthy should always be a high priority, whether it is better to suffer with an illness than to end our life, whether deformed children should be permitted to live – then, suddenly, one opinion is as good as another. We look to economists to calculate the costs and benefits of a speed limit of fifty-five miles per hour or the likelihood that increased government spending will fuel inflation. But who will teach us whether lives saved or time saved has moral priority, whether it is better that the old should have their savings destroyed by inflation or the young their future prospects diminished by lack of jobs? Advertising experts can make us want to buy almost anything. Who will teach us how many electronic games it is good to have?

If virtue can be taught, it must be a kind of knowledge. Surely, though, it is not simply the knowledge of technical expertise. A good bit of our confidence about the teaching of virtue stems, no doubt, from our success in teaching expertise. With Socrates we want to believe that morality is not mere opinion, that virtue can be taught. But clearly, if virtue is knowledge and can be taught, it must be a knowledge quite different from the expert's mastery of technique. What kind of knowledge is the knowledge-that-is-virtue?

The Knowledge That Is Virtue

Of the knowledge-that-is-virtue Plato affirms several things which seem to us at best paradoxical, at worst obviously mistaken. He holds that the virtues are not many but one and that a person who truly knows what is good will certainly do it. We, by contrast, are inclined to think that it is quite possible to be courageous but also unjust, that many times when we know what would be good to do we fail to do it because of our own moral weakness, and that sometimes perhaps we know what is good and deliberately set ourselves in opposition to it. In coming to understand the knowledge-that-is-virtue we may also begin to unlock the truth in Plato's puzzling claims.

The *Republic* is a great treatise on education. It culminates in the education of the philosopher-kings, outlined in Book VII. And beyond any doubt the high point of that seventh book is the myth of the cave (514a-517c). Socrates explicitly offers this myth as "an image of our nature in its education and want of education." The human beings in the cave are there from childhood, bound in such a way that they can look only in front of themselves. Behind them a fire burns, between them and the fire is a path along which statues of people, animals, and various objects are carried. The human beings who have been bound from birth see only the shadows cast by the fire from the objects carried along the path and hear only the sounds of the carriers. These shadows and echoes are, they believe, reality. Some of them become quite adept at distinguishing among the various shadows, and there are "honors, praises, and prizes for the man who is sharpest at making out the things that go by." But such technical expertise does not provide the needed deliverance. It comes only when a person is released and "suddenly compelled to stand up, to turn his neck around, to walk and look up toward the light." This turning will be painful, for it is a turning from the world to which we are naturally attached. But the one who turns gradually comes to see the things whose shadows he had seen before and begins to look at the light, even if it hurts his eyes. Even then the turning is not complete. One must get out of the cave and see the sun. Someone must, Socrates says, drag this poor soul away by force along the rough, steep path out of the cave and into the light of the sun. And once out of the cave it would still be a long time before anyone could actually gaze at the sun.

What we learn from this myth, Socrates says, is that we cannot put sight into blind eyes. "Education is not what the professions of certain men assert it to be. They presumably assert that they put into the soul knowledge that isn't in it, as though they were putting sight into blind eyes" (518c). But this is not the case – at least not when knowledge of the good is our concern. Rather, the power to see is in the soul, but "the instrument with which each learns . . . must be turned around" (518c). What moral education requires therefore is not an art of procuring sight but an art which can bring about this turning. "It was clear to Plato that virtue could not be 'transmitted' either by precept or by example."[6] We cannot put sight into blind eyes; we cannot put virtue into those who lack it. We must, it seems, be virtuous before moral knowledge can be ours. Paradoxical as it may seem, that is what the myth teaches us.

How then shall moral education take place? Plato's conclusion, unlike that of many today, is not that we should simply present people with moral problems and permit them to decide what their own value system will be. That approach perhaps takes seriously Plato's belief that the power to see is in the soul and cannot be inserted by the teacher, but it fails completely to appreciate how seriously he believes that "the instrument with which each learns . . . must be turned around." To ask those who sit bound in the cave what they see is an exercise in futility. They may have firm opinions. Some may impress us with their expertise and appear deserving of praises and prizes. We may even be dazzled by the sheer brilliance of argument as different men and women defend their opinions and choices. But at some point it will become clear that the arguments cannot be settled and that, though the arguments may seem impersonal and objective, they reflect not knowledge but preference or taste. When our notion of moral education is to ask those in the cave what they see, we forget, as

Iris Murdoch has written, that in "opening our eyes we do not necessarily see what confronts us. We are anxiety-ridden animals. Our minds are continually active, fabricating an anxious, usually self-preoccupied, often falsifying *veil* which partially conceals the world."[7] If knowledge of what is good can really be found, we will, it seems, need to take a longer way round to it than just asking each to inspect his soul and see what he finds there.

Much of the *Republic* is devoted to outlining the education needed for true virtue. If we combine what Socrates says about the education of the whole guardian class of the perfect city (in Books II and III) with what he says about the education of the philosopher-kings (in Book VII), we get a very lengthy process indeed.[8] Children are to receive training in music (which includes poetry) and in gymnastics – and, indeed, the contents of this education should be such that teach only right attitudes toward the gods and human virtue. Children may also begin to receive some instruction in the exact mathematical sciences. From about age eighteen to twenty they devote themselves to a physical training which includes military service. After that, those deemed suited are permitted to spend the years between twenty and thirty in studies which require exact mathematical knowledge (arithmetic, geometry, astronomy, etc.). These studies provide a propaedeutic for those permitted at age thirty to spend five years in the highest form of study: dialectic. From thirty to fifty they return to the practical life of the cave, and then at fifty they are at last "led to the end. And lifting up the brilliant beams of their souls, they must be compelled to look toward that which provides light for everything" (540a). They attain knowledge of the good itself – not merely a knowledge founded upon prior assumptions and hypotheses – and are prepared to rule in the city.

If we reflect upon this educational process outlined

in the *Republic*, we can learn about the sort of knowledge that, for Plato, is virtue.[9] When Socrates begins the myth to "make an image of our nature in its education and want of education," he says of the cave dwellers that "they are in it from childhood." The journey toward moral knowledge must begin then. Alasdair MacIntyre has written that in Greek, medieval, and Renaissance cultures "the chief means of moral education is the telling of stories."[10] In a similar vein Stanley Hauerwas has called attention to

> the contrast in style between Kant's way of doing ethics and works dealing with the spiritual life. For the latter, the use of examples is crucial, as they invite the reader to imaginatively take the stance of another as the necessary condition for the examination of their own life. Thus, for example, in William Law's *A Serious Call to Devout and Holy Life* . . . characters are created and discussed with almost the same detail as a novelist. Indeed, it may be for that reason that the novel remains our most distinctive and powerful form of moral instruction.[11]

Plato evidently agrees; hence, in Books II and III and Book X Socrates censors the poetry to which the young should be exposed. The fact that we are likely almost at once to react negatively to his proposal indicates, at the least, how different is our understanding of moral education. But if Plato is correct, if we cannot insert vision into the blind and if our environment shapes our perceptions and judgments of goodness, one whose vision of the good is not properly shaped in childhood may never come to see – except perhaps by "divine dispensation."

Thus, we have discovered one kind of teaching of virtue which is possible for human beings. It is not an imparting of actual knowledge of the good. It is only the telling of stories which transmit images and examples of moral virtue and in so doing begin to shape character by awakening a love for what is good. This provides not knowledge of the good but what Plato in his famous seventh letter describes as an "inborn affinity" for such knowledge (344a). And without this any other kind of instruction in morality is futile. The Athenian Stranger in the *Laws* makes the same point, that "the core of education . . . is a correct nurture, one which, as much as possible, draws the soul of the child at play toward an erotic attachment to what he must do when he becomes a man . . . " (643d). If this is achieved, if character has been molded by the right stories and good examples, when "rhythm and harmony most of all insinuate themselves into the inmost part of the soul," then says Socrates in the *Republic*, there is hope of coming to know what is good. Of such a youth Socrates says that

> due to his having the right kind of dislikes, he would praise the fine things; and, taking pleasure in them and receiving them into his soul, he would be reared on them and become a gentleman. He would blame and hate the ugly in the right way while he's still young, before he's able to grasp reasonable speech. And when reasonable speech comes, the man who's reared in this way would take most delight in it, recognizing it on account of its being akin. (401e-402a)

Here then we have a kind of moral training which – though we might today be tempted to call it "pre-moral" – is essential if we are ever to get out of the cave. We must learn to delight in what is good.

There is another kind of teaching, essential to Plato's program, which does not look much like the teaching of ethics. In the *Meno* Socrates and Meno discuss how we acquire virtue. In the course of the conversation Socrates develops his view that knowledge is remembrance and, as an illustration of this, elicits a geometrical proof from a slave who knows no geometry.

What shall we conclude? F. J. E. Woodbridge offers a suggestion worthy of consideration.

> You can teach Meno's slave geometry, but you cannot teach the sons of Pericles virtue. Socrates does not say that in words, but the 'Meno' says it in effect and says it more clearly than it says anything else. Geometry can be taught under the most unfavorable conditions, but virtue cannot be taught under the most favorable. That is Platonic doctrine.[12]

It is no accident that the propaedeutic studies – all involving mathematics – bulk so large in the *Republic's* educational scheme. If we want to teach morality, Plato seems to say, we must begin by teaching something else.

Why mathematics? We can begin to answer this question if we note why, according to Socrates, the study of dialectic must be postponed until approximately age thirty. To study dialectic is dangerous; for it involves the examination and testing of all which one considers certain. From childhood, Socrates notes, certain convictions were ingrained in us – convictions about what is just and good. We know that some follow different ways, but we do not consider that we might be mistaken. But if before our character is settled we examine philosophically our beliefs about justice, when we study argument and counterargument, finding each in turn seemingly persuasive, we may easily conclude that in these matters there is only opinion, not knowledge (538c-e). We may become skilled debaters, but we have lost the passion for truth. Socrates describes the result in two sentences which provide an apt characterization of much education also today.

> Then when they themselves refute many men and are refuted by many, they fall quickly into a profound disbelief of what they formerly believed. And as a result of this, you see, they themselves and the whole activity

of philosophy become the objects of slander among the
rest of men. (539c)

We must, Socrates and Glaucon agree, do all in our
power to prevent this. They also agree that "one great
precaution" is "not to let them taste of arguments while
they are young" (539b).

It is better, first, to study mathematics. And we
can now, I think, see why. The minds of those whose
character is just being formed Plato will not have us
flood with moral conundrums about which there will
seem to be only opinions—each as seemingly persuasive
as another. Instead, he recommends a kind of study in
which some certainty seems possible, in which doubters
can perhaps be persuaded and agreement reached.
Woodbridge is on target when he writes of Plato: "He
would not have teachers ask: What is *your* opinion?
What do *you* think? How does it impress *you*? How does
it *seem* to *you*?"[13] That is to say, the student should first
be introduced to disciplines in which personal opinions
do not seem to count, studies in which we must learn
simply to give ourselves to the facts, whatever they may
be and whether we like them or not. "For as the habit
of being led by what one studies to disinterested decisions grows, the soul grows more and more immune to
vanity, to self-deception, and to despair. It becomes
catholic, liberal, and generous. A soul may not be taught
virtue, but it may be prepared for it through habits of
disinterestedness."[14]

We have now two steps in the teaching of virtue
which do not look much like teaching ethics: inculcation
of character traits in the young by stories which elicit in
them a love for what is good, and the study not of ethics
but of other disciplines in which a reasonable certitude
seems possible and in which disinterestedness is
necessary. Clearly we have here a program intended to
develop in us a capacity for what Iris Murdoch has called

"*attention* to the world," i.e. "a just and loving gaze directed upon an individual reality." Such attention, Murdoch says, is "the characteristic and proper mark of the active moral agent."[15] And if we have lost the sense that this is an important element in moral education, we may have lost something essential in our moral inheritance.

> In the moral life the enemy is the fat relentless ego. Moral philosophy is properly, and in the past has sometimes been, the discussion of this ego and of the techniques (if any) for its defeat. In this respect moral philosophy has shared some aims with religion. To say this is of course also to deny that moral philosophy should aim at being neutral.[16]

If we really want moral knowledge, not just interminable moral arguments which can in no way be settled, we will need a discipline which, negatively, begins to suppress that fat relentless ego and, positively, begins to develop in us a love for the good.[17] It is clear that the education Plato proposes in the *Republic* is addressed to both these needs and is intended to develop in us the capacity really to *attend* with our whole being to the claims of goodness. Of course, some do not want to see. Almost all of us do not want to see all of the time. Sometimes we prefer the shadows of the cave, especially if our sharpness at making out the shadows has won us any honor or praise.

All this, Socrates tells Glaucon, is but "a prelude to the song itself," the last step in which the good is fully known (531d). And if up to this point there has been precious little that looks like the teaching of ethics, we need not be surprised if the same proves true here at the end. To be sure, dialectic – the educational method appropriate at this last stage – involves the examination of argument and counterargument, but it does not culminate in proof in any ordinary sense. It culminates in sight. No better description is available than that of Plato's seventh letter.

> The study of virtue and vice must be accompanied by an inquiry into what is false and true of existence in general and must be carried on by constant practice throughout a long period . . . . Hardly after practicing detailed comparisons of names and definitions and visual and other sense perceptions, after scrutinizing them in benevolent disputation by the use of question and answer without jealousy, at last in a flash understanding of each blazes up, and the mind, as it exerts all its powers to the limit of human capacity, is flooded with light. (344b)

Thus, as Socrates says in the myth of the cave, "the last thing to be seen and that with considerable effort, is the *idea* of the good; but once seen, it must be concluded that this is in fact the cause of all that is right and fair in everything . . . and that the man who is going to act prudently in private or in public must see it" (517c).

At the end of this journey comes knowledge, not just opinion. Plato's answer to the problem of our own experience – the fact that moral argument seems interminable – is to suggest that we do not all enter the lists as argumentative equals. The good man or woman knows, and if moral argument never ends it is not because some do not know the truth but because others will not be persuaded. "It is Plato's regular teaching that character is not irrelevant, but determinative, either for veridical knowledge or for ignorance."[18]

Moral knowledge may therefore be said to be a kind of intuition, a vision grasped by the eyes of the soul. And because it is, we can understand why tendance of one's soul should have been a preoccupation with Socrates. This is not intuition as moral philosophers have sometimes discussed it in our century; it is hardly open to anyone or everyone. The knowledge it offers is self-evident, but not obvious. It is self-evident because it shines by its own light and is not deduced from any prior premise or set of premises. It is not obvious because it can be seen only by those who have undergone the painful shaping and transformation of character outlined by Plato in the *Republic*. Placed beside it and seen in its light our own talk of moral education may at times appear less than serious.

Throughout Plato is faithful to his central insight: knowledge of what is good cannot be put into the soul by the teacher. We cannot put sight into blind eyes. Rather, the soul must be converted, turned around, and then it will not need to be taught. It will see. Having discovered what sort of knowledge is the knowledge-that-is-virtue, we are in a better position to appreciate the paradoxes which Plato regularly associates with Socrates' discussions of virtue. Many of the dialogues suggest that all virtue is one and is some form of knowledge. This has always seemed puzzling. As Werner Jaeger notes, "in our moral experience there is no commoner observation than that an individual can be distinguished by the greatest personal courage, and yet be extremely unjust, intemperate, or godless; while another man can be thoroughly temperate and just without being brave."[19]

It is possible to respond in various ways to Jaeger's observation. Is the courage displayed by the terrorist true virtue? One might hold that it is not, that it is not courage to face danger for an evil cause. Or one might hold that it is courage, but in this case courage is not virtue.[20] Or one might note that only some virtues are intimately connected to particular motivational states. Generosity or kindness may require a certain sort of motive, a motive likely to involve other virtues as well. Courage, by contrast, need not involve acting from any particular sort of motive and, hence, may bring along fewer virtues in its wake.[21]

Yet all this seems to miss the chief point, which gets lost in a thicket of analysis. Virtue, Socrates says in the *Republic*, "would be a certain health, beauty and good condition of a soul, and vice a sickness, ugliness and weakness" (444e). It is quite possible, and not I think contrary to Plato's point, that we might at various stages of life have some virtues and not others – or have a number of virtues in differing states of development. The claim that all virtue is one is, rather, a claim not about stages along the way but about the end which human moral development ought to attain. That end is knowledge of what is good, and it cannot be attained by one whose soul remains in any way diseased. If the virtue of justice is not fully developed in the soul, there will be moments when we will see not what is, but what we want for our own sake to see. If we lack courage in some measure there will be times when our vision of the good is clouded by concern for our own well-being. Or, to consider a Christian virtue, if we fail in hope, we may turn aside just at the moment when – round the next corner – we would have seen.

Naturally, therefore, Werner Jaeger is correct when he reports our experience that the virtues often do not go together in ordinary human character. This is an interim report from some point along the way. But none of these virtues can be fully developed apart from the others, and there is an intelligible sense in which we may say that – until the end, a healthy soul, is attained – each virtue, in whatever state of development it may be, remains vice or (at best) "splendid vice."[22]

It may also now seem less paradoxical that Socrates and Plato should regularly assert that one who knows what is good will do it. Here again we must remember that genuine knowledge comes only at the end of an arduous process of personal transformation. The man or woman who knows what is good can only be one whose character has taken on the pattern of the virtues. We may depend upon such a person to enact the good he or she sees precisely because this seeing has not from the outset been a purely intellectual undertaking. Only those whose desires, passions, and emotions have been properly molded can see. They have disciplined the fat, relentless ego. And then, in turn, since their character is virtuous, there will be no conflict between what they see and what they do.

Retreat into Authenticity

We are products of an egalitarian age, and our initial reponse is not likely to be favorable to a view which suggests that moral argument can be resolved only by the good (who may be few), and that the good have not just opinions but genuine knowledge. Perhaps, of course, we need such a shock to begin to set us free from the cave in which we too live, "stuffed with secondhand opinions."[23] Nevertheless, it may be useful at this point to consider an alternative to the view I have been sketching, an alternative to the view that moral knowledge is a kind of vision available only to those of good character.

In a wide-ranging, fascinating book Richard Rorty has recently mounted an offensive against the notion that knowledge (any knowledge, though here we are concerned with moral knowledge) is a matter of "seeing" the truth.[24] The very idea that our knowledge claims require "foundations" Rorty ascribes to "the Greek (and specifically Platonic) analogy between perceiving and knowing" (p. 157). He argues that we should abandon this search for "an unshakable foundation" and seek at best only "an airtight case" (p. 157). The proper metaphor to use with respect to knowledge is not that of *vision* but, instead, that of *conversation*. To know is to have "a right, by current standards, to believe" (p. 389); to say what is true is simply to be able to defend what you say against all comers in the ongoing conversation which is culture (p. 308). An "objective truth" cannot really be anything other than a bit of knowledge about which there is general agreement (p. 337).

If philosophy is no longer to provide foundations for knowledge, what role shall it play? It becomes for Rorty, in a paraphrase of Michael Oakeshott's metaphor, one voice in "the conversation of mankind." In moving to this perhaps more modest understanding of philosophy's role, Rorty distinguishes between two styles of philosophy – systematic and edifying philosophy.[25] Systematic philosophy involves the concerted effort to know – and to investigate the grounds upon which we can claim to possess "justified true beliefs, or, better yet, beliefs so intrinsically persuasive as to make justification unnecessary" (p. 366). The edifying philosopher, by contrast, is skeptical about any such claims to knowledge, seeing them as little more than "attempts to close off conversation" (p. 377). The edifying philosopher is interested less in "expressing a view" than in "participating in a conversation" (p. 371).

For Rorty, systematic philosophy is, I think, a futile attempt to transcend the limits of our historical location. More important, however, it becomes clear that he regards the impulse which generates much systematic philosophy as morally deficient. The systematic philosopher, dominated by the metaphor of knowledge as vision, ineluctably thinks of "having our beliefs determined by being brought face-to-face with the object of the belief" (p. 163). That is to say, the systematic philosopher holds that our beliefs are determined by confrontation rather than conversation (p. 163). For such a philosopher knowledge is as unavoidable "as being shoved about, or being transfixed by a sight which leaves us speechless" (p. 376). And it is here that Rorty discerns what we may call a moral defect. The systematic philosopher is in flight from responsibility – unwilling to accept the need for choice among competing views (p. 376). By contrast, the edifying philosopher turns out to be a heroic figure, one who "does not join in the common human hope that the burden of choice will pass away" (p. 376). To think that our minds can actually confront and know some objective truth is to imagine that the world is not something alien, something which requires us to choose our attitudes toward it and descriptions of it (p. 376). This is, Rorty suggests, to attempt to escape from our humanity and see ourselves as God (pp. 376f.).

This is a powerful attack upon the Platonic position I have sketched. Perhaps, however, we should try to tell the story a little differently than Rorty does. Perhaps it is Rorty (and the edifying philosophers upon whom he draws here) for whom the world is not alien. For what Rorty has lost is the sense of the world as creation – a world knowable (because created), yet unfathomable in its depths (because created). Josef Pieper states the alternative nicely.

> Because things come forth from the eye of God, they partake wholly of the nature of the Logos, that is, they are lucid and limpid to their very depths. It is their origin in the Logos which makes them knowable to men. But because of this very origin in the Logos, they mirror an *infinite* light and can therefore not be wholly comprehended. It is not darkness or chaos which makes them unfathomable. If a man, therefore, in his philosophical inquiry, gropes after the essence of things, he finds himself, by the very act of approaching his object, in an unfathomable abyss, but it is an abyss of *light*.[26]

If we see the world as created, we may not regard it as "alien" to ourselves, but we will certainly see it as other than the self, resistant to our projects. By contrast, it is for Rorty (and Sartre, upon whom he relies at this point) that the world is not alien. Rorty speaks of choosing our attitudes toward and descriptions of the world. Behind this language lies the belief that the world is malleable by the human will, that there is in it nothing which human freedom cannot determine, that it cannot finally resist our projects. It would be impossible in Rorty's world to "live a lie" – a possibility which depends upon a world resistant to our projects, a world to which we may improperly refuse to conform. Instead, Rorty must leave us with a vision of a world in which the greatest virtue will turn out to be authenticity – being true to oneself, accepting without bad faith the burden of choice and bearing it nobly. The world shrivels like a dried apple: instead of all created things bathed in an unfathomable abyss of light, we have a self being true to its own light for no reason other than that it is its own.

Indeed, the problem goes still deeper – as the self retreats not only from creation but from the Creator. Rorty suggests that the systematic endeavor to know objective truth is an attempt to escape our humanity and be God. Instead, he believes, we should content ourselves with keeping the conversation going. Rorty and the edifying philosophers (as he reads them) are therefore "agreeing with Lessing's choice of the infinite *striving* for truth over 'all of Truth'" (p. 377). Once again, this attitude has about it an air of grandeur, but then, so does Milton's Satan. If the seeker after truth is attempting to escape our humanity, it is a secularized humanity we are well rid of. For Rorty's notion of a human being depends on the belief that the human heart could never rest in God. Any moment in which the heart might rest would be described as an attempt to close off conversation. Any moment in which we were confronted by moral truth which demanded that we shape our projects to conform to it would be a moment in which the self became simply an object rather than a subject. Yet surely it is this human being who is always shaping and fashioning his world who is trying to be God—who, even if presented with the beatific vision, might well try to keep the conversation going rather than simply adore. This is, I think, the sort of human being Rorty's standpoint implies, and no one need fear being accused of seeking to escape the human condition so described. Some things it is wise to escape.

The image of conversation, delightful as it is, needs placing in its own historical location. Its proper place is not in "culture," still less in "mankind." One need only read Oakeshott thoroughly to realize that the metaphor has its roots in the experience of universities like Oxford and Cambridge—great places no doubt, but rare enough to make one doubt the value of letting such a metaphor shape a whole philosophy. Oakeshott says of a university what Rorty wants to say of life: "A university is not a machine for achieving a particular purpose or producing a particular result; it is a manner of human activity."[27] A university, he writes, "is a conversation . . . . A conversation does not need a chairman, it has no predetermined course, we do not ask what it is 'for', and we do not judge its excellence by its conclusion; it has no conclusion, but is always put by for another day" (p. 425). What a university offers, therefore, is "a moment in which to taste the mystery without the necessity of at once seeking a solution" (p. 426). "The characteristic gift of a university is the gift of an interval" (p. 426).

This is, to my mind at least, a splendid image of a university. Indeed, the chief defect of many of our universities today may be that both faculty and students want solutions to society's problems rather than an interim in which to "taste the mystery." Whatever may be the truth of that view, however, we should not forget that Oakeshott himself suggests that the metaphor cannot always be generalized. "It belongs to the character of an interim to come to an end; there is a time for everything and nothing should be prolonged beyond its time. The eternal undergraduate is a lost soul" (p. 426). Life is not merely an "interval," and conversation not always genteel. Sometimes, perhaps especially in matters of morality, we need to know the truth, not just be skilled participants in a conversation. When it comes to trying to raise a child, for example, a little moral knowledge may be far more important to us than "free and leisured conversation," however dazzling. We do not want our children to be "lost souls" and, hence, we are not permitted the luxury of being "eternal undergraduates." And only truths which themselves resist our projects in the world will be there for us to hang on to when we need them.

The image of conversation, enticing though it may be, suggests that "objective truths" are simply those on which we have (for the present) general agreement – a suggestion which will not deal kindly with those whose moral claims fail to persuade many others. And if to say what is true is simply to be able persuasively to defend what we say against all others in the ongoing conversation of mankind, one who has been released from the cave and gazed upon the sun is not likely to speak much "truth" when he returns once again to the cave.

> "Now reflect on this too," I said. "If such a man were to come down again and sit in the same seat, on coming suddenly from the sun wouldn't his eyes get infected with darkness?"
>
> "Very much so," he said.
>
> "And if he once more had to compete with those perpetual prisoners in forming judgments about those shadows while his vision was still dim, before his eyes had recovered, and if the time needed for getting accustomed were not at all short, wouldn't that be the source of laughter, and wouldn't it be said of him that he

went up and came back with his eyes corrupted, and that it's not even worth trying to go up? And if they were somehow able to get their hands on and kill the man who attempts to release and lead up, wouldn't they kill him?"

"No doubt about it," he said, (516e-517a)

Nevertheless, we might do well to worry less about keeping the conversation going and more about stopping and listening to him.

The Danger and Defect of Moral Education

Plato is concerned not just with the final goal – the vision of the good – but with the educational process which leads to it. But the goal is important and is, in Socrates' words to Theatetus, "becoming like the divine so far as we can" (176b). It is no wonder the way to such an end should be arduous, painful, and long. But the philosopher is not one who *has* wisdom but one who *loves* it and will settle for nothing less. We can learn from Plato whether we are serious about this love. If we are, he suggests, we will not think that "teaching ethics" should wait until students are old enough to determine their own character. Nor will it evince seriousness if we simply present children and students with case studies designed to help them clarify their own feelings and values; for at best that may help them to be among the adept who win honors and prizes in the cave. We can learn from Plato that we do not stand on neutral moral ground, that sometimes moral argument may be fruitless, not because it is only a matter of opinion, but because our character and commitments help to determine what we see. In short, for Plato the goal is nothing less than holiness, likeness to what is good. That quest never ends in human life, that aspiration always leads us on, and therefore to tend one's soul is always important.

And we must understand that, although no person can see for another, the journey toward this vision cannot be made in isolation. It must be made within a community which molds and shapes us in such a way that we delight in what is good.

At this point – and only when we take Plato seriously enough to reach this point – we must note the structural flaws in his program of moral education. They are chiefly two – one political and one religious in character. No one can claim to be at the end of the process Plato outlines. We never reach a point at which the Good ceases to draw us on toward a closer approximation to holiness. We must all give our reports from different points along the way – which means, from vantage points which affect our vision of what is good. If our own moral education is never complete, our knowledge remains partial. It may still be knowledge; to know a part of the truth is not to know what is only partly true. But the limits we face require that we leave room for different visions along the way. Plato himself recognizes this in the *Republic*, which is "the greatest critique of political idealism ever written."[28] The genuine philosopher who has left the cave and gazed upon the sun must go back into the cave and rule if the city is to be perfect. Socrates clearly says as much while seeming to ignore the fact that this is contrary to the philosopher's own desire. He at least cannot be happy in the perfect city – and therefore, it cannot be perfect. The philosopher turns out to be not the perfect citizen but one who transcends the limits of the perfect city and the claims of citizenship. And hence, if we are not to stifle the philosophic *eros* which yearns for the Good (or the restless heart which longs for God), our city cannot be that perfectly constucted republic but must be one which leaves place for differing visions of what is good. The requirements of ethics and of politics are never in perfect harmony.

The issue is nicely raised in the *Meno*, which begins with Meno's question to Socrates: "Can you tell me, Socrates – is virtue something that can be taught? Or does it come by practice? Or is it neither teaching nor practice that gives it to a man but natural aptitude or something else?" (70a). Thus, at the outset we are presented with three possibilities. Virtue may be learned through teaching; it may be learned by practice or habituation; it may simply fall to some as a natural aptitude.

In the course of the dialogue the first and third of these possibilities are eliminated. Virtue is not simply ours by nature, since it is a kind of knowledge which must be acquired (89a). But on the other hand, virtue cannot be learned by teaching, since there are no successful teachers of it (89d-e). The first and third alternatives are set aside, but nowhere in the dialogue does Socrates consider the second possibility – that virtue might be learned by practice, that for example we might become habituated to virtuous behavior through imitating the behavior of worthy exemplars. Instead, Socrates and Meno are forced to turn in the end to a "solution" not fully satisfactory. They decide that right opinion rather than knowledge may be sufficient for virtue. The right opinion about how to reach a goal – so long as it *is* right – will be just as good as knowledge of how to reach the goal. The defect of right opinions when compared with knowledge is that, like the statues of Daedalus, right opinions won't stay put. Lacking the certainty of knowledge, they are easily altered (97a-98a). Hence, those who have right opinion about virtue are fortunate indeed; for they have it only by "divine dispensation" (100a). If at any time there should come among those with opinions about virtue someone who truly knows,

> he would be among the living practically what Homer said Tiresias was among the dead, when he described him as the only one in the underworld who kept his

wits—"the others are mere flitting shades." Where virtue is concerned such a man would be just like that, a
solid reality among shadows.(100a)

That is, such a man would be like the philosopher who
had looked upon the sun but then returned to the cave.

Why does Plato not seriously consider the second
alternative—that if virtue is neither naturally acquired
nor taught, it might be learned by practice? We may say
that this alternative is represented in the dialogue by
Anytus. He is a "decent, modest" Athenian, elected to
many offices, who brought up his son with care (90a-b).
He would not dream of sending his son to the sophists,
who profess to teach virtue, and he is quite clear about
his preferred alternative to their teaching. If Meno
wishes instruction in virtue, "any decent Athenian
gentleman whom he happens to meet, if he follows his
advice, will make him a better man than the Sophists
would" (92e). That is to say, Anytus contends that virtue
is transmitted by "practice"—it is learned from the example of others in a well-ordered society.

Why cannot Plato consider this possibility directly
in the *Meno*? Not, I think, because it will not work. To
some degree, at least, virtue can be transmitted in the
manner Anytus suggests and the *Republic* articulates.
Virtue can be inculcated in the young. But a society
which takes seriously its need to do this will be a dangerous place for any Socrates to live. Indeed, Anytus gives
Socrates a thinly veiled warning.

> You seem to me, Socrates, to be too ready to run people
> down. My advice to you, if you will listen to it, is to be
> careful. I dare say that in all cities it is easier to do a man
> harm than good, and it is certainly so here, as I expect
> you know yourself. (94e)

A culture which seriously attempts to inculcate habits of
virtue in the young cannot easily permit its moral norms

to be transcended by other visions of the good. It must find profoundly disturbing – perhaps even dangerous – anyone who, like Socrates, functions as a "stingray," numbing and perplexing those (like Meno) who think they know what virtue is (80a-b). Such temporary perplexity may have helped Meno's slave boy learn a useful lesson in mathematics. Socrates suggests that the "numbing process" will be just as useful for those who seek to learn of virtue, but the *Meno* and the *Republic* – read as complete dialogues – are far more ambivalent.

Successful moral education requires a community which does not hesitate to inculcate virtue in the young, which does not settle for the discordant opinions of alternative visions of the good, which worries about what the stories of its poets teach. In short, there can be little serious moral education in a community which seeks only to be what we have come to call "liberal." For moral education requires that virtuous exemplars be presented the young, not that a thousand choices be given. At the same time, the goal of moral education – vision of what is good – can never be fixed in advance by any education, as if there were teachers who could regularly and easily transmit it. People must be left free to seek it, and that pursuit may shatter the confines of even the perfect city and make moral education difficult. Communities which seek simply to remain "open" and do not inculcate virtuous habits of behavior will utterly fail at the task of moral education. Communities which do not permit the virtues they inculcate to be transcended by what is good will ultimately cut themselves off from the very source which inspired their efforts to shape character. Perhaps communities which seek seriously to inculcate virtue while also gathering regularly to confess their failures and recommit themselves to what is good are the best we can manage. We recall that Plato's Academy was a community which assembled at fixed times to offer sacrifice.[29]

The first structural flaw in Plato's program of moral education I have characterized as political. The other is, if anything, even more deeply embedded. An obvious difficulty in Plato's program is that

> genuine philosophers are to be both the producers and the products of the right education. "Train up a child in the way he should go and when he is old he will not depart from it." But who can so train him? Why! those who have been so trained."[30]

In other words, Plato might have labored mightily to bring us no farther than Socrates' suggestion in the *Meno*. In order to get the program off the ground a "divine dispensation" would be needed. The need for grace goes considerably deeper, however. Indeed, Robert Cushman does not hesitate to describe this need as the central problem for Plato's *therapeia*, his program of moral education.[31] Who will lead us out of the cave? The question is not easily answered, since, by Plato's reckoning, the cave is of our own making. If we do not see what is good, the failure is not only in our intellect. We are ignorant because, at some fundamental level of our being, we do not want to see. That willful ignorance is, of course, opposed by the philosophic *eros*, the yearning for good which draws us. Hence, to be in the cave is to be torn between two possibilities. But it seems that our delight in the shadows of the cave – our own creation, after all – is the stronger pull. In the myth, we may recall, Socrates does not suggest that the cave dwellers manage to turn themselves around. He speaks of one who is "released and suddenly compelled to stand up, to turn his neck around, to walk and look up toward the light" (515c). At the slightest glimpse of the light he turns and wants to fall, for it hurts his eyes. And therefore, Socrates says, he must be "dragged . . . away from there by force along the rough, steep, upward way" (515e).

The entire program of moral education which the *Republic* sketches can offer no guarantee that we will not, in the end, prefer to remain willfully ignorant. Even at the highest levels – when inculcation of habits of virtue and mathematical training have done their work – dialectic may not be powerful enough to enable us to take that last step and attain the vision of the good. All Platonic dialectic can do is bring to consciousness the contrary pulls we feel. "The real question is how long a man can endure unresolved contrariety in his own spirit."[32] Not forever, we may speculate, but there will always remain two ways to bring that "contrariety" to an end. We can turn to the good or remain within the cave.

"The central theme of Platonism regarding knowledge is that truth is not brought to man, but man to the truth . . . . "[33] There is much to be learned about ethics and moral education from this central theme much that is preferable to our own current wisdom. And it seems correct to say that the truth cannot be brought to us, if that requires putting sight into the eyes of those who are blind or transmitting knowledge of the good to those who do not love it. Perhaps, however, the truth can be brought to us in other ways – in a way which, by drawing us with a love stronger even than Plato's philosophic *eros*, can overcome the division in our being and thereby transform our character. The possibility of any fundamental advance beyond Plato's program of moral education depends upon the possibility of such grace.

4. Instructing the Conscience

Some Contemporary Views
of Moral Education

"As it was taught in the American colleges in the nineteenth century, moral philosophy was in fact frankly exhortative, intended more to instruct the conscience than to stimulate the intellect."[1] That sentence from D. H. Meyer's *The Instructed Conscience* reminds us that there was a time when I might not have begun my ethics classes by emphasizing that it was a matter of little concern to me that the students and I should agree about the moral problems we study. It is a high calling to seek to "instruct the conscience" of the student. Most of us, for a variety of reasons, settle for trying to "stimulate the intellect."

The results of this choice may leave us dissatisfied, however. For example, Mark Lilla – concerned about the way public policy professionals learn ethics but with insight into the way many others learn it as well – has suggested that "they are learning a rather peculiar sort of philosophical discourse which allows them to make sophisticated excuses for their actions."[2] Ethics becomes a new casuistry dealing with difficult moral dilemmas. We think about these dilemmas, apply different ethical theories to them, and learn how "to be shrewd." But life is not like this, Lilla suggests. The moral life is not first and foremost theories and dilemmas but "a set of virtues."[3] What we need is not a theory to justify any decision but a set of moral habits, a way of life. That is, we need an instructed conscience.

If we attempt to instruct the conscience we assume that it needs shaping and disciplining. We assume that a moral education is insufficient which simply stimulates the intellect and encourages the student to express, articulate, and clarify the values to which he currently inclines. How different this is from Iris Murdoch's view to which we have referred earlier. "In the moral life the enemy is the fat relentless ego. Moral philosophy is properly, and in the past has sometimes been, the discussion of this ego and of the techniques (if any) for its defeat."[4] But Murdoch is a student of Plato. It should not surprise us if her suggestion differs from some current theories of moral education.

Clarifying Values

As one example of what passes for current theory we may consider the following statement from a widely used text on Values Clarification:

> If a child says that he likes something, it does not seem appropriate for an older person to say, "You shouldn't like that." Or, if another child should say, "I am interested in that," it does not seem quite right for an older person to say to her, "You shouldn't be interested in things like that." If these interests have grown out of a child's experience, they are consistent with his or her life. When we ask children to deny their own lives, we are in effect asking them to be hypocrites.[5]

The technique which grows out of this approach is intended to replace older, less effective, perhaps objectionable methods of moral education. In particular, it is offered as a replacement for (1) *moralizing*, which tries to tell others what values they should adopt, and (2) *modeling*, which attempts to transmit values not by precept but by example.[6] It may be useful to begin by considering a point most of us might be inclined to accept.

We are likely to agree that it would be bad to ask our children to be hypocrites. And yet, perhaps part of learning morality may be likened to a story

> about someone who had to wear a mask; a mask which made him look much nicer than he really was. He had to wear it for years. And when he took it off he found his own face had grown to fit it. He was now really beautiful. What had begun as disguise had become a reality.[7]

Such a story, which takes quite seriously our need to discipline the "fat relentless ego," suggests that we need to rethink the easy assumption that hypocrisy is bad. Or, perhaps better, we need to question the wisdom of equating moral disciplines (such as moralizing and modeling) with invitations to hypocrisy. Must we – at the risk of being hypocrites if we do otherwise – simply articulate, affirm, and prize whatever values we are inclined to hold? If so, character development can only mean coming to greater clarity about our present inclinations. It cannot include change, much less radical transformation, of those inclinations.

The theory of Values Clarification suggests what almost any conscientious parent knows instinctively to be wrong: that to ask or require another person to behave in a way contrary to his present inclinations is to ask him to be a hypocrite. Can this really be correct? It is hard to imagine that anyone could think very long about our use of the word 'hypocrisy' and conclude that telling a child "You shouldn't like that" was asking the child to be a hypocrite. It may not be the most successful way to undertake moral education, but it is hardly a call for hypocrisy. It is, rather, precisely what it appears to be: an admonition to try to control and channel one's behavior and, thereby, begin to alter one's character.

Feelings are not always subject to our immediate control. Overt behavior more often is. Such an admonition is simply a recommendation that we put on a mask – not with any intention to dissemble, but in the hope that we may gradually begin to look more like the mask, in the hope that our feelings may gradually conform to our behavior. Or, to use Aristotle's language, in the hope that we may begin to develop proper habits of behavior and become persons whose inclinations are not at war with such virtues.

Seeing this, we suddenly realize what an extraordinarily optimistic view of human nature is presupposed by Values Clarification technique. For example, Simon and deSherbinin, suggesting that modeling is an ineffective method of moral education and that teachers' energies should be directed to a better method, write: "Values clarifiers believe, however, that people who go through the process of deciding what they value will in the end reflect the ways one would hope, in any event, that all good teachers would behave."[8] Why should we suppose that, if only we learn to think clearly and consistently about our values, we will become such exemplary individuals? Why not suppose, on the contrary, that such a technique may develop consistent, energetic, effective thieves and cheaters? To put the question this way is to see that Values Clarification is, in essence, a modern though truncated version of the view that the virtues are one. That is, if we really achieve the virtues of clarity and consistency in our values, all other virtues must be present as well. What makes this a truncated version of the classical thesis is that in this modern version there is no slow, arduous process of transformation. Instead, it is available to anyone willing to undertake a few classroom exercises, and it requires only clarity about our character, not moral change. Because this is true, most of the depth is lost from Socrates' genuinely provocative thesis concerning the unity of the virtues. The Values Clarifiers may perhaps help us to get clear about the shadows we see on the wall of the cave. But they seem to have little interest in helping or – we hesitate to use the word Plato does – compelling us to stand up, turn around, and walk toward the light. No place here for souls in bondage needing to be set free. No place here for St. Paul's belief that clarifying our values, taken by itself, will only uncover a will divided between good and evil – and that, therefore, more than clarity will be needed.

Why would anyone espouse such a theory of moral education? The answer, I think, lies in our fear of indoctrination, a word at least as bad as 'hypocrisy' in our moral vocabulary. If we think we ought not – legally or morally – engage in moral indoctrination, we may be drawn to a method like Values Clarification which professes to leave everything in the student's value system intact while bringing this system to self-conscious clarity. It offers the alluring possibility of moral neutrality. Of course, we may have difficulty specifying the meaning of 'indoctrination,' and until we can say what it is we are not likely to know whether it is desirable. To that problem we return below. The possibility of moral neutrality can be dealt with more easily. It may, after all, be possible to avoid any objectionable indoctrination without professing moral neutrality.

In a helpful article, Richard Baer has pointed out that the technique of Values Clarification cannot be morally neutral.[9] This is not necessarily bad, of course. It is bad only if we think our method is morally neutral when in fact it is not. Baer notes that Values Clarification, as a teaching technique, relies on the asking of certain questions (e.g., "How did you feel when that happened?") to call attention to morally significant features of our behavior. And he notes that this in itself will make moral neutrality impossible. Certain aspects of our behavior are singled out as morally important, and thereby a moral judgment is made. He offers a conversation like the following to make his point:

> Student: "Yesterday I poured blue paint all over my cat."
>
> Teacher: "How did you feel when that happened?"
>
> Student: "I felt terrible. I should have used red paint."
>
> Teacher: "No. I meant, how did you feel about getting paint all over the cat?"
>
> Student: "Oh. I felt terrible. I shouldn't have done anything to harm my cat."[10]

An overly simple exchange, certainly, but we see the point. For the questioning technique to work, the teacher must instruct, not just clarify. The very fact that the teacher must call attention to morally significant features of action is itself instruction – which cannot be done from morally neutral ground. The teacher has pointed out what he regards as important in the student's experience. Indeed, even at a considerably more advanced level of instruction no selection of "important" moral problems or theories can be made from morally neutral ground. This will be just as true of attempts to "stimulate the intellect" as of efforts to "instruct the conscience."

The trick, then, is not to be morally neutral but to avoid whatever constitutes objectionable indoctrination. Consider one possible definition of indoctrination.

> It is the *deliberate* attempt at *directly* affecting the value system *without* either preliminary or collateral legitimation to the recipient . . . , the classic examples being subliminal advertising, some variants of brainwashing, religion for toddlers, and lobotomies. The "integrity of the person" must be respected by the educator, and should be respected by the parent, as early as possible; it is that respect which requires that there be explanation, justification, and permission before tamper-

ing with values. . . . [M]oral education for pre-rational children must be absolutely minimal, preferably reversible, and its content must be culturally, not parentally, legitimated.[11]

This statement correctly recognizes that our methods of teaching ethics must change as children grow. One does not teach a college ethics class in the same way one teaches a four-year-old. Nevertheless, if we taught all four-year-olds according to this prescription – or, perhaps we should say, failed to teach them, since this prescription makes questionable even very simple forms of parental nurture – college ethics classes might become even more chaotic than they already are. Aristotle wrote that "to be a competent student of what is right and just, and of politics generally, one must first have received a proper upbringing in moral conduct."[12] His point is a simple one. Only those in whom some of the basic moral attitudes have been developed – who are disposed to act honestly, speak truthfully, prize fairness, esteem courage, honor parents, care for the weak, plan for descendants, delight in mercy – can profit from a more systematic and sophisticated study of ethics. If we seek to stimulate the intellect of those whose conscience is not yet so instructed, we may teach them to be shrewd but little more than that. Indeed, only if some of these basic virtues have already developed can we profit from thinking about the "hard cases" of moral life. If we have not learned the most elementary rules of baseball, we will never reach the point where we need agonize over the wisdom of walking a batter intentionally. Similarly, if we are not (for example) characterized by the trait of truthfulness, we will not be in a position even to recognize certain moral dilemmas.

Any advanced instruction in ethics depends, therefore, on a prior inculcation of basic moral attitudes. Acquiring moral principles is not just learning to reason in certain ways, nor it is simply attaining clarity about what we think. It is coming to feel certain ways and being characterized by certain habits of behavior. Especially for young children, these basic moral virtues are not devoloped by reasoning; on the contrary, they provide the indispensable foundation for all future moral reasoning.

It may seem, then, that we are left with the alternatives of (a) indoctrination, or (b) letting children and students arrive at their own moral values. Neither looks much like moral education. And in somewhat haphazard fashion we will probably tend to split the difference – "indoctrinating" young children (perhaps with a slightly guilty conscience), and refraining from any attempt to influence the moral attitudes of older students. Andrew Oldenquist, however, has offered a definition of indoctrination which suggests that there might be such a thing as necessary and good indoctrination about which no one need feel guilty.

> It seems reasonable to limit the term "indoctrination" to cover coercive and deceitful kinds of influencing – such as browbeating students, not permitting open discussion, lying about the controversiality or consequences of a principle, or slipping one's own moral views into clarifying discussions or the format of dilemmas while pretending to be non-directive and morally neutral. These are genuinely harmful things and deserve to be called indoctrination, or alternatively, bad as distinct from good indoctrination. The mistake of a good many writers on moral education is that they define "indoctrination" as teaching children that *anything* is right or wrong.[13]

Even in what is a generally excellent article, however, Oldenquist sometimes suggests that the justification for engaging in moral education ("good indoctrination") is that any society which has an agreed-upon core of moral

values must transmit these values or commit societal
suicide. And, of course, one could still ask, in response,
by what right we determine for young children or older
students that the survival of our society is of moral con-
sequence. Is not this value itself an arbitrary imposition
upon the student of what we deem useful?

The only answer to such a question which preserves
the possibility of a moral education that instructs the
conscience is to hold that those basic moral virtues which
we seek to teach – to act honestly, speak truthfully, prize
fairness, esteem courage, honor parents, care for the
weak, plan for descendants, delight in mercy – are not
simply chosen by us but are the foundation of all moral
reasoning. When, therefore, we seek to inculcate them –
which is quite a different thing from seeking rationally
to justify them – we do not impose our own moral creation on those who are younger and weaker than we. Instead, we seek to transmit the values which we recognize not as our choice or our creation but as our limit.
These are the values which ought to limit and discipline
our own fat relentless egos just as much as the egos of
those we teach.[14] To fail to see this is to be unable to
distinguish between indoctrination and inculcation.

The teaching of ethics at a relatively sophisticated
level – the sort that may go on in college courses – is,
therefore, dependent on a different sort of teaching.
The virtues must be inculcated in children, and they
must learn to love what is good and right. Only then will
they be in a position to think seriously about moral
theories and hard cases. Not clarity but character
should be the first goal of moral education. And even at
the more sophisticated level, we should not imagine that
careful examination of theories and dilemmas is a purely
intellectual undertaking. Admission to college or university is not a ticket out of the cave. There is no way out
except the long, arduous struggle, the disciplining of the
ego, by which we learn to love the good. We should

wonder, then, when we examine a list of goals for the teaching of ethics – such as that given in the Hasting Center's report on *The Teaching of Ethics in Higher Education* – and find little interest in the shaping of character. Indeed, that report quite straightforwardly says: "One goal frequently proposed for courses in ethics is missing from our list: that of changing student behavior. . . . We have concluded that this is not an appropriate explicit goal for a course in ethics."[15] But as long as we avoid the forms of "bad indoctrination" which Oldenquist notes, it is hard to know why we should agree with this conclusion. Caring about students' character, wanting them to be more than just shrewd, is a way of taking them seriously. It is also a frank recognition that moral argument is not just a game at which some are more skillful and win prizes and admiration. Even at this more sophisticated level, clarity is not the only desideratum; here, too, character may be a prerequisite for seeing certain truths. To spend a lifetime stimulating intellects loosely attached to uninstructed consciences is a vocation that ought to have little appeal.

Cognitive-Developmental Theory

R. S. Peters has called attention to the fact that our word 'education' may derive from either *educere* (to lead out and, thus, develop the potential already present) or *educare* (to train or mold, thus suggesting an external standard to be internalized).[16] A defect of Values Clarification as an approach to moral education is that it is committed only to clarity about one's character, rather than transformation of character; it seeks to educe but lacks any standard by which to measure clarified character. A considerably more sophisticated theory of moral education – in some ways akin to Values Clarification, but which seeks to bridge the gap between *educere* and *educare* – is the cognitive-developmental theory of Lawrence Kohlberg.

The kinship between this theory and Values Clarification lies in their common rejection of the view that moral development is the internalization of the external norms of one's society and their rejection of the view (which may have both psychoanalytic and Christian forms) that human nature, because of its destructive or evil propensities, needs to be shaped and disciplined. Unlike Values Clarification theory, however, Kohlberg believes he can identify a moral standard against which to measure moral development, and he has constructed a theory which directs our attention, not just to clarity about character, but to change of character. When he writes that a common tendency in much moral education is "to focus moral instruction on the trivial and immediate, rather than on the universal and important, because this approach gives rise to fewer headaches about . . . ethical justification," Kohlberg could well be marking one of the contrasts between Values Clarification and his own theory of moral education.[17]

Kohlberg's hypothesis – now supported to some extent by several decades of research – focuses on the developing powers of cognition in moral education. His central concern is with the *reasons* people give to support and explain their behavior. His assumption, explicitly stated, is that "we all, even and especially young children, are moral philosophers."[18] The moral reasoning of human beings develops quite naturally – though only when stimulated by social interaction – through a series of stages. These stages depict our progress as moral reasoners from a time when we think largely in egoistic terms, through a period when we conform to societal norms, to a time when we are able to reason morally in ways which seek universality and transcend the conventions of particular societies. We get, then, a sequence of stages which can be simply charted:

1. Preconventional Level

a. The person's reasoning is governed by a desire to avoid punishment – and hence is largely an attempt to obey authorities and avoid breaking rules.

b. The person now recognizes the value of reciprocity – of meeting others' interests and not just his own. But the importance of reciprocity still lies in the fact that it is instrumental to the person's well-being.

2. Conventional Level

a. The person now sees worth not just in satisfying his own interests but in meeting the expectations of others – here considered primarily as those to whom one has special bonds (parent, child, friend).

b. The person sees worth in meeting the expectations of others – here understood primarily in terms of the social order to which one belongs.

3. Post-Conventional Level

a. The person now reasons in a way which permits him to consider, not just fulfilling the duties of his place in society, but changing the social order by appeal to a principle which transcends that order – at this stage, chiefly the principle of utility upon which the social contract is itself based.

b. The person now reasons in accord with self-chosen moral principles of universal applicability. All particular moral rules are judged in light of such universal principles (which are purely formal in character). The most important such principle is not utility but justice (understood as including respect for the rights and dignity of all human beings).

It seems fair to say, then, that a world of people whose powers of moral reasoning were fully developed through all six stages would be a world in which inordinately large numbers of people sounded like Kant and Rawls.[19] One progresses – and we are to understand the stages as ranked in ascending order – from a level of moral reasoning concerned only with the particular individual through a level of reasoning concerned for the good of society (and the self as member of society) to the pinnacle of moral reasoning at which our focus is once again on the individual, but no longer a particular individual. At the highest stage one reasons in terms of the perspective of any rational individual – and, hence, in terms that can be universalized.[20]

Although Kohlberg often refers to the work of John Rawls in support of his theory, it is interesting to note that he also describes his position as "a reassertion of the Platonic faith in the power of the rational good."[21] If we note a few assumptions built into his cognitive-developmental theory we will understand why he might make this claim. The six stages of moral reasoning are "structured wholes." That is, people at any stage are fairly consistent in their reasoning when confronted with various moral problems. In fact, the stages are said to form an "invariant sequence." We may move through them at different speeds. We may even become fixated at some stage. But any movement is always upward through the stages; there is no jumping around, nor is there any skipping of stages. We are able to understand reasoning characteristic of stages lower than our own and reasoning at one stage higher than our own (else we could never move up), but reasoning more than one stage above our present level is likely to mean little to us.[22] The sense in which such a theory might be called Platonic is that the good, understood as a universal good transcending cultural particularities, is already known, needing only to be called forth by proper instruction . If our intellects are properly stimulated by a kind of Socratic questioning, movement upward through the stages is fostered. "Moral education is the leading of men upward, not the putting into the mind of knowledge that was not there before."[23] There is good reason to think, as we will see, that Kohlberg fails to capture important elements of Plato's view, but we can at least understand why he might claim some kinship.

The process by which one moves upward through the stages of moral reasoning needs examination. To consider it is to confront many of the most important features of the Kohlberg approach to moral education. Cognitive-developmental theory pictures moral education, not as the internalization of norms gotten from family and society, but as progress through the several stages of moral reasoning. Kohlberg is, however, unwilling to describe this as a natural unfolding of innate stages (as there may be, for example, in our biological development). The young child has "structuring tendencies" which, *together with* "environmental conditions necessary to facilitate moral development," produce progress through the stages.[24] Thus, not a natural unfolding but an interaction between cognitive structures and suitable environment is the prerequisite for moral development. We note in passing that this permits Kohlberg to make a claim similar to one we encountered in the theory of Values Clarification: The teacher is not transmitting "fixed moral truth" but merely offering a context which will stimulate the child to restructure his or her own experience.[25] What sort of environment will provide the needed stimulus?

> The first step in teaching virtue . . . is the Socratic step of creating dissatisfaction in the student about his present knowledge of the good. This we do experimentally by exposing the student to moral conflict situations for which his principles have no ready solution. Second, we expose him to disagreement and argument about these situations with his peers. Our Platonic view holds that if we inspire cognitive conflict in the student and

point the way to the next step up the divided line, he will tend to see things previously invisible to him.[26]

Evidently this "Platonic view" does not reckon with the fact that the student placed in this environment may simply become adept at winning prizes in the cave.

The stress on the cognitive and neglect of the affective dimension of moral behavior, and the relative optimism about human nature, suggest that Kohlberg has served up, at best, a pale imitation of Plato's view. Most striking of all – and most worthy of reflection – is this: The dialectic which Plato reserved for some thirty-year-olds who had already undergone intensive training of various sorts – that dialectic Kohlberg offers the grade-school child. Much of what Plato would offer the young child Kohlberg regularly indicts as a mere "bag of virtues" approach to moral education: exhortation to practice the virtues, along with stories validating these virtues, and adults to serve as exemplars of them.[27] Kohlberg is concerned to emphasize that moral and intellectual virtue are not different and that moral virtue does not come through doing, through habit. Instead, he takes himself to be following Plato in arguing that virtue is a kind of knowledge, and moral and intellectual virtue are not different in kind. Yet, the knowledge that for Plato was virtue was a knowledge acquired only at the end of a long process of education, a process specifically designed to discipline the fat relentless ego, a process which took seriously the affective dimension of human behavior. Socrates says in the *Republic* that only the youth with "the right kind of dislikes," who would "blame and hate the ugly" while still young, would be in a position to delight in reasonable speech about the good as he grew older (401e–402a). Hence, Plato's enormous concern about the stories the youth would learn to love. How different was Plato's concern – and his theory of moral education – we may judge by contrasting his approach (stories first, dialectic for the thirty-year-old) with Kohlberg's curt dismissal of the technique which has been used in countless hours of parental nurture: "The pat little stories in school readers in which virtue always triumphs or in which everyone is really nice are unlikely to have any value in the stimulating of moral development. Only the presentation of genuine and difficult moral conflicts can have this effect."[28]

What Kohlberg offers us, we can now see, is both a moral and a psychological theory. He suggests that the most satisfactory moral position is one which stands in the line running from Kant to Hare and Rawls. He also suggests – his psychological theory – that the development of moral reasoning, if properly stimulated, passes naturally from the lower to the higher stages (and here he pays homage to, while misunderstanding, Plato.) The two theories, moral and psychological, fit together nicely. Indeed, Kohlberg suggests that his moral theory is more adequate than alternatives for some of the same reasons his psychological theory is superior: Both are more integrated and differentiated than alternative views.[29] A moral theory built on the premise of universalizability offers a way to resolve the tensions and contradictions built into conventional levels of morality; it offers a way to resolve conflicts between moral rules. Similarly, his psychological theory suggests that we move from lower to higher stages of moral reasoning in order to overcome the cognitive conflict we suffer when we face the contradictions inherent in a lower level of reasoning. In short, the goal is equilibrium.[30]

Neither the moral nor the psychological half of this theory is entirely persuasive. We have already noted, in seeing how far Kohlberg is from Plato's position, something of what is mistaken in Kohlberg's psychological theory of moral development. In his stress on cognitive development and moral reasoning he forgets the affective side of our behavior. If he wishes to affirm, with Plato, that those who know the good will do it, he fails to see that for Plato only those who had first been trained in doing the good would be in a position to know it – and then, in turn, truly to do it in the fullest moral sense. In his emphasis on reasoning about difficult moral conflicts he fails to see that without some of the virtues we will be unable to recognize hard cases when we see them. The truth is no different here than it was in the case of Values Clarification theory. The intellect can be usefully stimulated only if the conscience has first been instructed. Only those who have learned to delight in the good, those in whom the basic moral attitudes have been inculcated, can profit from the presentation of difficult moral conflicts. The hard cases may only teach the un-instructed conscience how to be shrewd.

This is simply to note that moral education must in-terest itself at least as much in our dispositions, habits, and traits of character as in our reasoning. Kohlberg, while granting the distinction between moral reasoning and behavior, has suggested that one's reasoning stage is a good predictor of one's action.[31] The truth, not just of common sense but of research, suggests otherwise. "Don't assume that because people use high-level think-ing about hypothetical moral problems, they will use high-level thinking to solve real-life problems in their personal experience."[32] Thus writes Thomas Lickona, summarizing one of the lessons he says we have learned from research into moral education. The same insight, based this time upon experience of human nature, was nicely articulated by C. S. Lewis: "I had sooner play cards against a man who was quite skeptical about ethics, but bred to believe that 'a gentleman does not cheat,' than against an irreproachable moral philosopher who had been brought up among sharpers."[33]

The problems with Kohlberg's moral theory are legion.[34] One of the ways in which his theory seemed superior to Values Clarification was in its commitment not just to clarity about, but to change of, character. We may wonder, however, whether the view of morality adopted by Kohlberg achieves this. It is characteristic of theories which place heavy emphasis on universalizability to suggest that we try to adopt the perspectives of the various persons involved. But we do this not to ask what would be right for any of them. Instead, we do it to determine what we would find acceptable if we were that person. "A just solution to a moral dilemma is a solution acceptable to all parties, considering each as free and equal, and assuming none of them knew which role they would occupy in the situation. . . . A claim is final only if one would uphold it as final no matter which role in the situation one were to play. . . ."³⁵ Hence, I am to consider myself as filling the various roles involved and to ask what, *given my desires and inclinations*, I would find acceptable in those roles. But I do not specifically ask whether my desires and inclinations — my fat relentless ego — may perhaps need some reshaping. I ask, simply, what I would find "acceptable." Thus, "a universalizable decision is a decision acceptable to any man involved in the situation who must play one of the roles affected by the decision, but does not know which role he will play."³⁶ He gets clarity, it would seem, simply about what he is willing to accept.

Perhaps we are to assume that a genuinely sympathetic attempt to occupy the roles of several people in imagination will in fact bring about a reshaping of our inclinations. And that may sometimes occur. At least as often, though, it may happen that we simply do not *see* what is really required in these roles. "By opening our eyes we do not necessarily see what confronts us. We are anxiety-ridden animals. Our minds are continually active, fabricating an anxious, usually self-preoccupied, often falsifying *veil* which partially conceals the world."³⁷ This truth is missed in moral theories like the one Kohlberg adopts — which ask us to *see* what universalizability requires, what we would choose in an original position, what an ideal observer would approve. They miss the truth that vision depends upon character, that what we see may depend upon who we are.

What we see when we consider hard cases, how we respond to the moral dilemmas around which Kolberg's theory is built, depends on what we *care* about. Richard Peters is correct, then, to suggest that any theory of moral education must focus our attention here. "How do children come to care? This seems to me to be the most important question in moral education; but no clear answer to it can be found in Kohlberg's writings."[38] This question is especially important if we are to appreciate the role religious belief may play in morality. Craig Dykstra has argued persuasively that, by focusing on reasoning about moral dilemmas, Kohlberg's approach has missed the role that religious disciplines such as repentance, prayer, and service may play in shaping vision.[39] If the psychological half of Kohlberg's theory is deficient in failing to pay attention to affect, to how we move from reasons given to action taken, the moral half of his theory is equally deficient in failing to note that the dilemmas we perceive and, therefore, the reasons we think germane, depend upon our character. Dykstra captures both these deficiencies in his short formula: "action follows vision; and vision depends on character."[40]

As an example of how important this may be, in particular for religious believers, we can note the commitment of Kohlberg's theory to equilibrium. For Kohlberg the higher stages are relatively more satisfactory because, psychologically, they deal better with the anxiety caused by moral conflict and, morally, they better adjudicate the conflicts of individual and group interests. Thus, he suggests that "if a richer man gives all that he has to the poor, he has followed the Golden Rule but he has not arrived at an equilibrated solution."[41]

True enough – and no doubt ending on a cross is not what we should call an "equilibrated solution" either. All this means, however, is that anyone whose vision is shaped by Christian belief may not always value equilibrium as highly as Kohlberg's theory does. Suffering may be a necessary feature of the moral life, inextricably interwoven with the disciplining of the fat relentless ego – not always to be overcome in a higher, more integrated solution. Tragic dilemmas may sometimes have little hope of resolution in a world shaped and disordered by sinners, and we may have little confidence that moving to a higher stage of reasoning will deal adequately with all hard cases.

Indeed, the longer we think about the moral life the less certain we may be that Kohlberg really has his six stages in proper ascending order. His moral theory aims really at a certain kind of political justice which seeks the *lowest* common denominator morally in order to permit people with conflicting interests to coexist in society. It emphasizes only those goods which can be shared by large numbers of people. However necessary this may be politically, it is far from certain that such a universal justice must always have moral priority in our lives. We can see the effect of Kohlberg's theory if we notice how two proponents of his view explain the importance of moving from stage three to stage four reasoning:

> Whereas in stage three there is an attachment to persons, an appreciation of their motives, and a strong sense of loyalty, which makes one willing to overlook infractions, in stage four the law is seen as the ultimate guarantee of people's rights because it is the ultimate guarantee of social order.[42]

Moral progress is here equated with movement beyond personal loyalties and attachments, with loss of sensitive appreciation of the motives which lead particular people to act. Of course, that we may sometimes face choices between particular attachments and more universal obligations is clear. And that particular attachments must sometimes give way to larger considerations of justice is also clear. But that universality must always be purchased at the cost of personal loyalty is far from clear, although it is assumed in Kohlberg's theory.[43] The challenge to such theory is forcefully stated in E. M. Forster's famous statement:

> If I had to choose between betraying my country and betraying my friend I hope I should have the guts to betray my country. Such a choice may scandalize the modern reader . . . . It would not have shocked Dante, though. Dante places Brutus and Cassius in the lowest circle of Hell because they had chosen to betray their friend Julius Caeser rather than their country Rome.[44]

Such attachment to a friend could never count for much in Kohlberg's theory; it is at best stage three reasoning. And perhaps Forster is mistaken in plumping as he does for personal loyalty to one's friend. Nevertheless, it is instructive to note that the goods made possible by the *highest* stages of moral reasoning in Kohlberg's theory are *lowest* common denominator goods. Some of us, when attending to our world, might think them not always the most important for human life. We do not all see the world in the same way and, hence, do not always discern the same moral dilemmas in case studies presented to us. To Kohlberg this may seem a reaffirmation of the relativism he sought to overcome in his cognitive-developmental theory. But the affirmation that what we see depends on who we are need not result in such relativism; it is quite compatible with Plato's view that character must be properly shaped before we can see the *truth*, but that truth can be seen by the instructed conscience.

Nevertheless, once we put the issue this way it is clear that we are back to the problem Kohlberg sought to avoid: indoctrination. One of the attractions of his theory of moral education – an attraction for some at least – is that it suggests a possibility of "nonindoctrinative" moral education begun from neutral ground. "The attractiveness of defining the goal of moral education as the stimulation of development rather than as the teaching of fixed rules stems from the fact that it involves aiding the child to take the next step in a direction towards which he is already tending, rather than imposing an alien pattern upon him."[45] Since the six stages purport to depict only formal patterns of moral reasoning, no specific moral content or norms are being imposed. A "natural dynamic already in place" in the child is fostered but without the imposition of any particular moral scheme.[46] That, at least, is the claim.

This neutrality is, of course, largely spurious.[47] As we have seen, substantive moral commitments – and not E. M. Forster's – are embedded in the theory of stages, and a particular vision of what counts in the moral life is at work. This means that if, indeed, there really is some natural dynamic at work in the movement up through the stages, we might sometimes have moral reason to oppose that natural dynamic. More important, once the claim to moral neutrality is lost and the substantive commitments of the Kohlberg theory noted, its claim to be "nonindoctrinative" is jeopardized. If the system does not stand on philosophically neutral feet what is the justification for *imposing* this approach to moral education? The answer one will find in Kohlberg's writings, I believe, is that only this method is constitutionally acceptable. He believes that the commitment to justice enthroned in stage six is the commitment of our society. Even if that claim is true, however, it is one thing to foster the value of justice (as Kohlberg understands it) because our society is committed; it is quite another thing to foster it because in so doing we foster an objectively correct morality. To do the former is to do what many will call indoctrination, an act the strong impose on the weak; to do the latter is to inculcate a morality which binds us as well as those we instruct.

It seems, therefore, that we cannot seriously seek to instruct the conscience without making and seeking to impart substantive moral commitments. Moral reasoning depends upon first principles from which it proceeds, principles which must first be present as virtuous habits of behavior inculcated in the young. The dilemma, of course, is that in seeking to impart substantive virtues we may seem only to be choosing arbitrarily one "bag of virtues" and imposing it in the name of moral education. We may say that this "bag of virtues" is not simply our choice but is the moral truth which binds us too; nevertheless, to one who does not share our vision it will certainly seem otherwise.

We appear to be caught in a circle. Moral understanding depends on vision which depends on character; yet character can be shaped only in accord with a prior vision. This problem underlies the connection for Aristotle between ethics and politics; it leads him to conclude the *Nicomachean Ethics* by pointing to the *Politics*, by suggesting that the study of ethics cannot be complete apart from the more general problem of how best to constitute a political community. Thus, he concludes his *Ethics* by noting that before moral argument can be effective, "the soul of the listener must first have been conditioned by habits to the right kind of likes and dislikes . . ."(X, 9). Hence, the transition to politics. A character with the right kind of likes and dislikes can be fashioned only in a properly ordered, virtuous community. "To obtain the right training for virtue from youth up is difficult, unless one has been brought up under the right laws" (X, 9). Reason discerns moral truth only if the soul is rightly ordered; vision depends upon character. We need therefore to be brought up in a society which will teach us – by precept, example, and habit – to act virtuously, to have the right kind of likes and dislikes. Good ethics requires good politics, or so Aristotle would have it.

He is not depicting what we would call a liberal polity. He himself writes that "with a few exceptions, Sparta is the only state in which the lawgiver seems to have paid attention to upbringing . . ." (X, 9). And he may help us comprehend the difficulties of moral education within a liberal political community such as ours. Within such communities, unless there is already a far-reaching moral consensus, most attempts at moral education, Kohlberg's included, are likely to be either methods of indoctrination under the guise of moral neutrality or pale imitations of anything that might seriously be called moral education. With such alternatives we are perhaps well advised to forego public attempts at moral education; it can seldom be done properly within liberal polities. Instead, we should heed the advice of Aristotle, who wrote that if these matters are not cared for by the community "it would seem to be incumbent upon every man to help his children and friends attain virtue" (X, 9). We should, that is, recognize that in political communities like ours, communities which rightly have high regard for individual freedom and which – perhaps because they do so value freedom – lack much in the way of moral consensus, we should be frankly sectarian in our attempts at moral education. Each should help his children and friends strive for virtue as we fashion our smaller communities of belief and seek to transmit the vision which inspires us. In doing so we would be faithful both to our own liberal political structure and to Aristotle's insight about the difficulties such structures pose for moral education. And perhaps out of such sectarianism there will arise some smaller communities whose vision is so powerful and persuasive that new moral consensus will be achieved among us. If that should happen, it will for a time be possible to have serious moral education within a liberal polity – until, of course, that moral consensus too breaks down.

Moral understanding and action depend on vision; vision depends on character; character must be shaped by those who come before us. But what justifies their claim to a vision of moral truth? By whom was their character shaped? Aristotle must find a good lawgiver, Plato a philosopher-king, Kohlberg a moral expert. We do not, I think, produce such people naturally. We can transmit only the corrupted human stock, with its distorted vision, which is ours. Our need therefore exceeds our powers. What moral education requires is a revelation by which we can test our vision and a grace powerful enough to transform our character. Good ethics, it turns out, will require not just good politics but good theology.

5. The Examined Life
Is Not Worth Living

Learning from Luther

For Christian theology there can be little doubt of the authority of the Bible. Even if we stress the authority of the sovereign God or the risen Christ, the language Christians speak about God and the beliefs they affirm about Christ have their root in the scriptural word. Even if we emphasize the centrality of Christian experience, that experience is itself shaped by Biblical narrative and teaching. Even if we seek to learn from and respond to the needs of our world, we view and interpret that world through the prism of the Bible. Even if we emphasize the indispensability and authority of the Church's tradition, it is still a tradition that seeks to unfold and develop what is conveyed in the Biblical record.

To say that the Bible is an authority which the Christian theologian must heed is not to say that this authority can solve all theological difficulties or by itself provide an answer to every question. It would be almost as true, in fact, to say that many of the important theological problems are raised by the Bible. They become problems precisely because, found in an authoritative text, they must be taken seriously by Christians. Without such authorities we have few difficulties; we think whatever we please. But to submit one's reflection to the authority of the Bible is to confess a willingness to consider certain issues as problems just because the texts raise them. Something like this is true of Christian reflection about virtue.

Perhaps no book of the Bible has been more constantly is use among Christians than the Psalms. Important in the liturgical life of the ancient Hebrews, it has been no less significant for Christians. Used regularly in the Church's worship, a source of inspiration for much Christian prayer and poetry, often committed to memory – the language of the Psalter has been of inestimable influence in Christian piety and theology. It is, therefore, of some importance to consider the image of human virtue which many of the psalms convey.

> Who shall ascend the hill of the LORD?
>   And who shall stand in his holy place?
> He who has clean hands and a pure heart,
>   who does not lift up his soul to what is false,
>   and does not swear deceitfully.
> He will receive a blessing from the LORD,
>   and vindication from the God of his salvation.
>   (24:3-5)[1]

The virtuous human being is one who can with some confidence stand before God, one whose character can withstand the penetrating judgment of the Almighty.

"Thou hast upheld me because of my integrity, and set me in thy presence for ever" (41:12). Here again is the authentic voice of many a psalmist, the affirmation that it is virtue which fits one for entry into the divine presence. And this affirmation, in the mouth of one who seriously proposes to pursue such virtue, can suggest a confident self-mastery which even God must recognize.

> Vindicate me, O LORD,
>   for I have walked in my integrity,
> and I have trusted in the LORD without wavering.
> Prove me, O LORD, and try me;
>   test my heart and my mind. (26:1-2)

Even more striking is the sense the psalmist sometimes conveys that there is no hidden corner of the self in which vice lurks, the confidence that he can see himself, as it were, with the eye of God.

> Hear a just cause, O LORD; attend to my cry!
> Give ear to my prayer from lips free of deceit
> From thee let my vindication come!
> Let thy eyes see the right.
> If thou triest my heart, thou visitest me by night,
>   if thou testest me, thou wilt find no wickedness
>   in me; my mouth does not transgress.
>   . . . .
> My steps have held fast to thy paths,
>   my feet have not slipped. (17:1-3,5)

Reading these and similar psalms we might wonder how the Psalter could have played such a prominent role in Christian prayer and worship. Such a confident affirmation of meritorious achievement might seem inappropriate on the lips of those whose central affirmation is, "While we were yet helpless, at the right time Christ died for the ungodly" (Romans 5:6). From this perspective any virtue we possess can hardly amount to a righteousness which would fit us to stand before God. St. Paul writes that Christ died for the *ungodly*. If, therefore, we can stand in God's presence, it is because in Christ God has come to sinners and shown himself willing to count Christ's virtue as their own.

One might respond by suggesting that virtue in the New Testament must be something quite different from virtue in the Old Testament. In the psalms we have cited virtue involves self-mastery and such development of character as makes us fit to withstand God's judgment. In the passage from Romans virtue means our acceptance by God for Christ's sake. However, to set Old and New Testaments against each other in this way would

be mistaken; for there are other voices and accents in
the Psalms than those we have noted thus far.

> When our transgressions prevail over us,
>> thou dost forgive them.
> Blessed is he whom thou dost choose and bring near,
>> to dwell in thy courts!
> We shall be satisfied with the goodness of thy house,
>> thy holy temple. (65:3-4)

Here the psalmist does not stride confidently into the
presence of God; he is conscious of being forgiven,
chosen, brought near by God. He is satisfied not with his
integrity but with the goodness of God's house. Again in
Psalm 51, a penitential psalm often used by Christians,
the psalmist recognizes that God desires "truth in the inward being" (v. 6) and that such an inner virtue must be
God's work. "Wash me thoroughly from my iniquity, and
cleanse me from my sin" (51:2). In Psalm 17 we found
a confidence of freedom from any hidden vice; in Psalm
19 we find a recognition that we can never see ourselves
as God does – whole and entire. "But who can discern his
errors? Clear thou me from hidden faults" (19:12). For
the writer of that verse there can be little confidence
that we *possess* virtue; instead, we live in hope.

> If thou, O LORD, shouldst mark iniquities,
>> LORD, who could stand?
> But there is forgiveness with thee,
>> that thou mayest be feared.
>
> . . . .
> O Israel, hope in the LORD!
>> For with the LORD there is steadfast love,
>> and with him is plenteous redemption. (130:3-4, 7)

The most casual examination suggests, then, that it
would be far too simple to play off Old against New
Testament. On the contrary, a Christian theologian ex-

amining the concept of virtue, who acknowledges the Bible's authority and wants his thinking to reflect that acknowledgment, now has a problem. He must come to terms with two seemingly different understandings of human righteousness. He must ask whether human virtue consists in the gradual development and mastery of character traits the goodness of which even God must admit, or whether our virtue is simply that a forgiving God dwells with us even in our sinful condition.

To be a person of good moral character is not merely to have certain virtues, though it is that; the idea of character suggests something less piecemeal, a fundamental determination of the self for which the agent is to be praised and for which he can take a certain amount of credit.[2] This suggests that nothing could be more important than that we should – like Socrates – tend the soul and examine our life. Thinking about virtue directs our attention inward upon the self and its capacities for self-mastery and self-realization. The stability that comes with development of character – and characteristic behavior – may suggest that virtue becomes a possession of the person who has achieved such self-mastery. Yet, as we have already noted, some central Christian affirmations challenge this emphasis upon the examined life, suggest that it may ultimately be self-defeating, and hold that not self-mastery but grace is the prerequisite for virtue.

The same ambivalence appears if we focus upon *development* of character. One of the recurring themes in the literature of moral education is that, if character involves habitual behavior, it can be developed by a kind of moral exercise. Our being is shaped by our doing. By hitting the baseball often enough I may become proficient at it. Similarly, by facing danger regularly I may become courageous. There are, of course, alternative theories – Rousseau disliked habit about as much as Aristotle recommended it – but it is hard to deny that all our efforts at moral education draw on the importance of habit to some degree. Yet, there is a gap between the deed and the person, between habitual behavior and character. Facing danger regularly may teach me to discipline the inclinations which urge me to flee, but can it guarantee that I stand firm not because I fear the shame of being branded a coward but because I love the good I defend? This seems to call for a more fundamental transformation of character, and it is not clear that any amount of doing can create such being.

To see what is theologically at stake here we will examine how one theologian dealt with the concept of moral virtue, attempting to take seriously its two quite different meanings. For Martin Luther the issue we have posed was of central importance, and we might summarize the central theme of his theology as a claim that the examined life is not worth living. We will consider two of his writings: his treatise "Against Latomus," and his exposition of Galatians 3:10-14 in his magisterial 1535 Galatians commentary. We see in these writings what a theological analysis of moral virtue requires, the central issue it raises. In both writings Luther subjects an ethic of virtue to serious theological challenge; the examined life is given its place, but only within a larger context in which divine grace rather than human virtue is preeminent.

Two Models of the Moral Life

In 1519 Luther's writings were condemned by the theologians of Louvain, a condemnation to which Luther replied in the following year. In 1521 one of the Louvain theologians, known as Latomus, published a defense of the original condemnation – to which Luther in turn responded in his treatise "Against Latomus."[3] A good bit of the argument turns on several propositions

affirmed by Luther and denied by Latomus: that sin remains in the Christian even after baptism, and that
every good work done by a Christian while still in this
life is sin. Of these two the latter is obviously the
stronger and, on the face of it, more paradoxical claim.
We can begin with it.

Part of the debate involves the question of how properly to interpret certain biblical references. We need not
rehearse the intricacies of this debate, but it is worth
noting an example in order to appreciate the case Luther
is prepared to press. In Ecclesiastes 7:20 we read that
"there is not a righteous man on earth who does good
and sins not." Our first inclination might be to suggest
that this means simply a kind of commonplace truth: No
one manages never to fall into sin. Everyone falls short
somewhere along the way. Luther insists however – and
we will not worry here about the adequacy of his ex-
egesis – that the passage makes a stronger claim. It
says, he holds, that a righteous person sins even when
doing good. There is no one "who sins not when he does
good" (p. 183). Our good works are not in his view an entirely "spurious righteousness"; they are good "before
men" and in the forum of our own consciences (pp.
173ff.). But they cannot stand the divine judgment;
hence "our good works are not good unless His forgiving
mercy reigns over us" (p. 172).[4]

This is Luther's famous anthropological maxim:
that the Christian is *simul justus et peccator* – simultaneously saint and sinner. And here this maxim does not
mean: partly saint / partly sinner. It means entirely
saint and entirely sinnner – and both at the same time.
Our deeds, taken in themselves and subjected to divine
scrutiny, must be seen as the deeds of a sinner. But seen
as the deeds of one who is "in Christ," they are the actions of a saint with whom God is well pleased. It is
worth noting that one of the reasons Luther holds this
view is because he thinks not just in terms of acts but in

terms of character. He is constantly concerned not to isolate the deed from the person, to evaluate not individual slices of behavior but the total self. The fruit exhibits the nature of the tree, he says, using a favorite example (p. 209). And again, "a man doing good is a subject which has sin as its attribute" (p. 187). One could scarcely ask for a greater emphasis upon *being*, not just *doing*. This might be said, in fact, to be the old thesis of the unity of the virtues, stated now in the categories of Reformation theology.

At the same time it is true that the way in which Luther stresses *being* is not conducive to some of the central themes of an ethic of virtue. For what one is, one's being, is determined by the divine verdict. That verdict admits of no gradations—one is either a sinner (when seen and judged in oneself) or a saint (in Christ). And it makes good sense of a sort to say that one is purely passive before this divine verdict. Here there is no stress upon self-realization, much less self-mastery. Virtue is not in any sense one's possession; it is simply a verdict of Another upon whom one must rely. Any stable characteristics which a self may display, any continuities within one's character, are relatively unimportant. They are characteristics of a subject "which has sin as its attribute." Life is not the gradual development of a virtuous self; it is a constant return to the promise of grace. The examined life, if honestly examined, will reveal only that the best of our works are sin—for the fruit exhibits the nature of the tree. And indeed, as Luther thought he had learned from personal experience, too much attention to the examined life can be dangerous; it directs our gaze inward rather than outward to the promise.

The *simul justus et peccator* maxim, taken as literally as Luther sometimes means it, leaves little place for the concerns of an ethic of character. The whole of life is taken out of the human agent's hands by the divine verdict, and there is no real space left for judgments about gradual development of character. The divine judgment is an either / or pronouncement made upon the person, not just upon particular deeds or traits. Yet, even Luther could not always talk this way. There were things he needed and wanted to say which required a different understanding of what it means to be *simul justus et peccator*. There were moments when for Luther this meant: partly saint / partly sinner— moments when he had to recognize that the unity of the virtues was a goal of life, a present reality only in hope.

We can see this when Luther argues against Latomus that sin remains in the Christian even after baptism. Latomus' claim is that after baptism there may be *imperfection* but not *sin* in the Christian. Luther holds that sin remains in the Christian but no longer *rules* the Christian. He wants only to insist that this remaining but not ruling sin should still be called by its proper name. When we call it sin we make clear that it still warrants God's condemnation and that we must flee to the promised grace. Thus he can write, still very much in the either / or mode:

> You will therefore judge yourselves one way in accordance with the severity of God's judgment, and another in accordance with the kindness of His mercy. Do not separate these two perspectives in this life. According to one, all your works are polluted and unclean on account of that part of you which is God's adversary; according to the other, you are genuinely pure and righteous. (p. 213)

The interesting thing about these sentences is that they combine the two different ways of understanding the *simul justus et peccator* maxim. There is a "part" of the Christian which is God's adversary and a "part" which is not—the partly saint / partly sinner model. But since God judges whole persons, not just deeds or character traits, the Christian is also entirely saint (in Christ) and entirely sinner (in himself).

We may notice, however, that only the one way of talking – partly saint / partly sinner – can make place for an emphasis on development in the moral life. Luther, still thinking and talking both ways, says that baptism removes the *power* of all sins but not their *substance*. "The power of all, and much of the substance, are taken away. Day by day the substance is removed so that it may be utterly destroyed" (pp. 208f.). "Day by day" – here there is room for gradual development of character, room for the Christian's assault, aided by grace, upon the fat relentless ego, room even for the self-mastery which makes progress in virtue possible.

In a very clear and well developed section Luther sets forth both ways of talking (pp. 223f.). We can chart his position in the following manner:

God's two ways of dealing with sin

	Law reveals	**Gospel reveals**
the person viewed "in parts" (doing)	corrupt nature	gift of infused faith
the person viewed whole (being)	wrath of God	grace of God

God deals with sin in two ways – through law and gospel. These two divine verdicts each reveal something about our human nature and something about God's judgment on that nature.

In the law we learn the corruption of our nature.

We come to recognize the sinful impulses which lurk within us. This does not mean that we see no good in ourselves; it means only that we recognize the sin that is there and know our guilt. In the gospel, by contrast, we learn of and receive the gift of faith. This faith, which Luther is willing to call an infused gift, begins the internal process of healing the corruption of our nature. "Faith is the gift and inward good which purges the sin to which it is opposed" (p. 227). Faith is that "part" of the self no longer opposed to God, and it is committed to purging that other "part" which continues to be the adversary of God.

We see ourselves in part – both in the light of the law, which reveals our sinful nature, and the gospel, which infuses faith and begins the healing process. God, however, sees us whole. And the contrary judgments of God – judgments not just of deeds or virtues but of persons – we also learn in law and gospel. In the law we learn that God punishes sinners; we learn of his wrath. This is, Luther writes, more terrible than to learn the corruption of our nature; for this is not a partial verdict, not a verdict which finds something to praise and something to blame. Rather, the judgment of God's wrath is that there is "nothing profitable" even in what seems good in our nature (p. 225). Indeed, Luther specifically notes that this judgment applies even to our virtues – there is "nothing profitable" in our prudence, courage, chastity, "and whatever natural, moral, and impressive goods there are" (p. 225).[5] In the gospel we learn that God's grace is opposed to his wrath, that for Christ's sake he is wholly and entirely favorable toward sinners.

When we think in the first way – of our corrupt nature and the gift of faith which begins to heal that corruption – we can, without denying the importance of God's grace in this process, make room for progress and development in the moral life, room for the gradual achievement of moral virtue through effort and discipline, and room for the careful examination of our lives and "tendance of the soul" which Socrates commended. When we think in the second way – of the contrary divine verdicts of wrath and grace upon our whole person – there is room only for a continual return to the word of promise which assures us that the wrath of God has been overcome by his favor. The first model encourages us to think of life as a grace-aided journey and of virtue as a gradual possession which we may come to acquire through the moral discipline to which faith is committed. The second model encourages us to think of life as a perpetual dialogue between the contrary verdicts of wrath and favor, to see the self as passively determined by these verdicts, and to understand faith as the continual return to the promise that grace has triumphed. On the first model we may grow in faith as that "part" of us which is God's adversary is gradually purged. On the second model faith is always the same – a naked trust in the promise. Luther himself finally offers a marvelous summary of his position, a summary worth quoting at length.

> Now we finally come to the point. A righteous and faithful man doubtless has both grace and the gift. Grace makes him wholly pleasing so that his person is wholly accepted, and there is no place for wrath in him anymore, but the gift heals from sin and from all his corruption of body and soul. It is therefore most godless to say that one who is baptized is still in sin, or that all his sins are not fully forgiven. For what sin is there where God is favorable and wills not to know any sin, and where he wholly accepts and sanctifies the whole man? However, as you see, this must not be attributed to our purity, but solely to the grace of a favorable God. Everything is forgiven through grace, but as yet not everything is healed through the gift. The gift has been infused, the

leaven has been added to the mixture. It works so as to purge away the sin for which a person has already been forgiven. . . . In the meantime, while this is happening, it is called sin, and is truly such in its nature; but now it is sin without wrath . . . . To be sure, for grace there is no sin, because the whole person pleases; yet for the gift there is sin, which it purges away and overcomes. A person neither pleases, nor has grace, except on account of the gift which labors in this way to cleanse from sin. God saves real, not imaginary, sinners, and he teaches us to mortify real rather than imaginary sin. (p. 229)

From either vantage point grace is essential for virtue. From the perspective of the first model grace is necessary as an enabling power, infusing the gift of faith which struggles against sin. From the perspective of the second model grace is necessary as a pardoning word, which sees the sinner whole in Christ and therefore sees him as virtuous.

What is at stake here – both for Luther and for our own understanding of an ethic of virtue? Luther himself recognizes that many might regard his dispute with Latomus as mere verbal disagreement (p. 236). Latomus says imperfection remains after baptism; Luther says sin remains; both agree that what remains does not condemn the believer in Christ. Why then all the shouting? Because, I think, each sees danger in the position of the other. Latomus finds in Luther one who imperils the examined life, who – because he brands everything as sin – is unable to take seriously the small disciplined steps by which virtue struggles to root out vice from the Christian's life. Luther – while granting the importance of this daily, bit by bit struggle – finds in Latomus one who fails to see that selves, not isolated deeds or character traits, are what count before God. Luther speaks of sin, not just imperfection, in the Christian in order to make clear that any hope a person may have before God must lie in the undeserved favor of God. All the particular deeds and the developed virtues we may claim do not add up to a righteous *person*. And, perhaps paradoxically, Luther suggests that it is his position rather than that of Latomus which will foster true virtue. If we fail to see ourselves as God sees us, he writes, "we cheapen Christ's grace and minimize God's mercy, from which necessarily follows coldness in love, slackness in praise, and lukewarmness in gratitude" (p. 240). That is, the virtues of love, praise, and gratitude are fostered precisely to the degree that we do not try to foster them but, instead, look outside ourselves to the promised mercy. The examined life is not worth living – not only because it can give the conscience no peace before God but because it does not really issue in virtue. When we stop trying to tend our own soul, when we hand that soul over to God and realize that we cannot bring our virtue to God but that he must (in Christ) bring virtue to us, then we experience a kind of liberation which makes possible true virtue, the virtue which comes not from the slow, disciplined transformation of character through development of virtuous habits but from the liberating acceptance of the sinner by a loving God.

This is Luther's fundamental claim. We may perhaps be struck by the fact that, however different the language, the claim is not unlike an understanding of virtue whose pedigree extends back at least to Plato. Plato's thesis that the virtues are one is essentially the observation that character is not a matter of bits and pieces, not a matter of isolated virtues and vices. That thesis is paradoxical, as is Luther's language, but both see a deep truth about virtue. Both see that our virtues are *ours* – and that if the self is not whole, the virtue is specious. Where Luther and Plato differ, the difference lies primarily in the fact that Luther goes farther. Plato's entire system of education sketched in the

Republic is intended to discipline the soul and bring a person out of the cave and toward the vision of the Good. Yet, even at the highest level of Platonic dialetic there remains a gap. The person is brought toward the Good as his character is gradually shaped and disciplined, but the shaping is in bits and pieces while the person is not. Hence, there always remains a question whether dialectic is powerful enough to help a person see the Good. Our attempts to develop virtue can be only partial, piecemeal. But, as Plato realizes, really to see and love the Good, one must already be virtuous. It is not clear, therefore, how the gap which separates being from doing can be bridged unless—as Luther thought had happened—the initiative should come from the side of the Good itself. "God in his grace has provided us with a Man in whom we may trust" (p. 235). And so, having been made virtuous in that man, we now love virtue. All our doings, all our bit by bit progress, could not bridge the final gap, could not create a being wholly dedicated to virtue. The tree cannot be made healthy by spraying the fruit. Thus Luther against Latomus: However much piecemeal progress toward virtue we sinners make, ours is still the virtue of sinners—hence, sin. First the person must be virtuous. *We* may develop worthy traits of character; only the divine initiative can create a virtuous self. Character depends finally not upon self-mastery but upon a moment in which one is perfectly passive before God.

Dangers of the Examined Life

Luther's theological standpoint is not just unintelligible paradox. It answers to a deep need in any ethic of virtue. It recognizes our inability to get from virtues to virtue, from traits of character to a transformed self. We should not forget, however, that Luther speaks in two ways. His theology in its most radical moments might suggest that moral education is futile, that the only worthwhile "moral education" would be a constant return to the promise of divine grace, that there could be little point in the development of virtuous habits of behavior since these could never eliminate the need for divine initiative. Why not, then, simply start with and constantly return to that divine initiative? Why bother ourselves with virtues and the gradual shaping of character?

But Luther does bother. In the treatise "Against Latomus" he had bothered. He had written of gradual progress in faith, of gradually purging that "part" of the self which is God's adversary. We can see again how important it is for Luther to speak in both ways if we consider a small portion of one of the masterpieces of his mature theology, the 1535 Galatians Commentary.[6] In expounding Galatians 3:10 Luther notices something peculiar in St. Paul's argument. Paul writes that "all who rely on works of the law are under a curse." As support for this claim he cites the Old Testament passage "Cursed be every one who does not abide by all things written in the book of the law, and do them." Peculiar support, one is inclined to think. The Old Testament passage says that anyone who fails to do what the law requires is cursed. And on the basis of that passage St. Paul claims that all who rely on doing what the law requires are cursed. We might suppose that St. Paul can move from

Anyone who fails to do what the law requires is cursed.

to

All who rely on doing what the law requires are cursed.

only by means of some concealed premise such as

No one can do fully what the law requires.

Luther, however, makes a different interpretive move. The move suggested above would imply that *if* anyone could in fact do fully what the law requires, he would be in a position to rely on his doing of the law. The only reason one should not rely on it is because none of us can meet the law's requirements. For Luther, however, the problem goes deeper than this. To "do" what the law requires while relying on this "doing" for one's standing before God would not in fact be to do what the law requires. Any true doing of the law calls for faith in the mercy of God, and such faith cannot be present when we rely on our virtue. Thus Luther writes:

> There are two classes of doers of the Law. The first are those who rely on works of the Law; against these Paul contends and battles in this entire epistle. The second are those who are men of faith. . . . (p. 253)

And again:

> Therefore "to do" is first to believe and so, through faith, to keep the Law. For we must receive the Holy Spirit; illumined and renewed by Him, we begin to keep the Law, to love God and our neighbor. (p. 255)

And once more, picking up a metaphor prominent in "Against Latomus":

> But because there are two sorts of doers of the Law, as I have said, true ones and hypocrites, the true ones must be separated from the hypocrites. The true ones are those who through faith are a good tree before they bear fruit and doers before they do works. (p. 257)

Thus, when we read in the Old Testament, "Cursed be every one who does not abide by all things written in the book of the law, and do them," the *doers* who, it is implied, will not fall under the curse are true doers, what Luther calls "theological doers." Their doing presupposes faith.

True virtue is, therefore, not possible as a human achievement; it cannot be thought of in terms of self-mastery. Indeed, it requires once again that moment of naked faith in which the self is perfectly passive before God. Our vices, Luther writes, have their source in our refusal

> to be justified by a divine blessing and formed by God the Creator. It [our hypocritical self] refuses to be merely passive matter but wants actively to accomplish the things that it should patiently permit God to accomplish in it and should accept from Him. And so it makes itself the creator and the justifier through its own works. . . . (p. 259)

Even the language of "theological doing" is slightly suspect and easily misunderstood. The faith which is presupposed by all theological doing of the law is a gift, the creation of God. It is naked trust in the promised favor of God, trust abstracted from all consideration of our deeds and virtues.

> Refer doing to the Law, believing to the promise. As widely as the Law and the promise are distinct, so far apart are faith and works—even if you understand "doing works" in a theological sense. . . . [For] the Law, whether it is done morally or theologically or not at all, contributes nothing whatever to justification. The Law pertains to doing. But faith is not of this sort; it is something completely different. . . . (p. 272)

The faith of which Luther speaks here quite clearly admits of no development over time. It is not a virtue gradually developed and strengthened bit by bit. It is a mathemetical point: the self passive before God—and the self a self, whole and entire, only because it is so passive before God.[7]

When we compare this discussion with "Against Latomus," written almost fifteen years earlier, we must say that, if anything, Luther has sharpened and intensified his emphasis upon the divine initiative. And this in turn suggests still greater urgency for our question: Why concern ourselves with virtues and the gradual shaping of character? Our being – which is wholly the work of God – precedes any doing. What place, then, for character formation?

Luther seems relatively unperturbed by the problem. "Christians do not become righteous by doing righteous works; but once they have been justified by faith in Christ, they do righteous works" (p. 256). That is his view. And yet, the very next sentences suggest that he is quite aware of the alternative understanding of virtue and willing to grant it a limited place. "In civil life the situation is different; here one becomes a doer on the basis of deeds, just as one becomes a lutenist by often playing the lute, as Aristotle says. But in theology one does not become a doer on the basis of works of the Law; first there must be the doer, and then the deeds follow" (p. 256). This theme recurs throughout his exposition of Galatians 3:10-14. Philosophical doing and theological doing must be clearly distinguished. The former seeks to shape character through virtuous action. The latter holds that virtuous action is possible only if character has first been transformed. Philosophical doing is fine – in its place. But its place is emphatically not to determine the status of the self before God, the persons we really are. It will do for everyday attempts to develop our own character or that of others; there doing may precede and shape being. But by itself it can fashion us only in bits and pieces; it can at best make us selves who are partly saint and partly sinner. Before God, who sees us whole, that is not enough; for God desires fellowship neither with deeds nor virtues but with persons.

We find, once again, that Luther seems simply to have two different ways of talking about our virtue and character. We could, without much difficulty, find similar distinctions in many of his other writings as well as the writings of other Christian theologians.[8] But there would be little point in continuing to pile up evidence. The point now is to try to understand why Luther seems compelled to talk in these two ways about virtue and to ask whether the two can be held together in one theological system.

When we consider human character, its virtues and vices, we seem driven to think both in terms of particular traits of character – delimited virtues and vices – and of character in a more general sense as a fundamental determination of the self.[9] And, if nothing else, Luther's willingness to speak paradoxically makes clear that these are quite different ways of thinking about the self. On the one hand, he displays what we may term a *substantive* understanding of virtue. Our virtues are traits of character which can be developed over time through habitual behavior. They provide the self with a certain continuity even in the midst of its growth and development. They suggest, when relatively well developed, a kind of self-mastery, a moral agent upon whom we may rely, who can be depended upon to display the virtues in his behavior. From this perspective a certain confidence in moral education – that attempt to shape being by doing – is warranted. Substantive virtues can be developed and sustained by those who take seriously the examined life. Once developed, the virtues are truly ours.

On the other hand, Luther displays what we may term a *relational* understanding of virtue. From this perspective the virtuous man or woman is simply one accepted by God; one upon whom the divine favor rests. We are not just bundles of deeds or virtues; we are men and women made for fellowship with each other and, ultimately, with God. We need to be loved and accepted, not just to have our deeds or virtues commended. Hence, 'character' may suggest not just particular traits but the person – the person who is not made to be an isolated monad but to exist in relation. And there is no way to get from particular traits of character, from any ensemble of virtues, to a person who is accepted. All our doings may shape our being, but we can never see the self we have made whole and entire. We may shape our being, but we can never create a self. We may make ourselves lovable, but we cannot thereby establish a relation with or claim upon God. If therefore we are to have character in the fullest sense, if the fundamental determination of our self is to be right, we must be willing to be passive before God. Renouncing our claims to self-mastery, recognizing that the self we are, wholly and entirely, is known only to God, we simply hear the divine Word which announces and thereby establishes a relation of love between creature and Creator. From this perspective our efforts at moral education are relativized – for what is needed is not development of virtues but a continual return to the divine initiative. Our efforts at moral education may add to our virtues, but they cannot bring about the relation that establishes our selfhood. And hence, one might say that the examined life is not worth living; for at its very best – which can be good indeed – it offers only an ensemble of virtues, not the relation we seek and for which we are created. Indeed, the examined life may even prove dangerous. Focusing our attention on our own self-development, we may, in the name of moral effort, lose that sense of liberation which true virtue requires. Focusing our attention on that sense of self-mastery which results from a serious attempt to shape being by doing, the examined life may lead us to think of virtue as a secure possession upon which we can rely.

Luther's view seems to be, then, that the examined life is necessary but not, finally, worth living – that we should make what progress we can in virtue but always without anticipating that it could make of us what we want to be. Can his two attitudes toward virtue form a coherent theological whole? If we think of virtues as substantive traits, we are thinking of the person as partly saint and partly sinner – as one who seeks to progress and develop in a way that will diminish the part that is sinner and augment that part of the self that is saint. If we think of virtue as a relation of acceptance before God, we are thinking of the person as simultaneously and entirely saint and sinner – in oneself a sinner, in Christ a saint – and as one who needs constantly to hear the divine word of favor. On the first model life is a journey, a gradual progress toward virtue. On the second, life is a continual return to that perfectly passive moment, that mathematical point in which the self is whole and wholly virtuous before God.

No one could deny that these two views stand in some tension. On the one hand, our substantive virtues may be few, yet we may be accepted and righteous before God. On the other, our substantive virtues may be many, yet if we rely on them we may lack the faith which *is* virtue before God. There need be, it would seem, little correlation between our virtue understood substantively and our virtue understood relationally. Indeed, Stanley Hauerwas has described just this as the "Protestant concern": to show that the actual shape of our life has no significance for our virtue (relationally understood).[10] How can one manage to speak of virtue in both ways?

In part, I think, the answer lies in the framework which the Christian story – beginning in creation and moving steadily toward a providentially determined end – supplies. The divine Word announces what we, caught up in the successive moments and piecemeal progress of our temporal existence, cannot see: that we are whole and wholly virtuous. But that same divine Word, spoken by the God who rules our temporal history, announces his own commitment to display one day the truth of his verdict. That is, God is committed to transforming people who are partly saint and partly sinner into people who are saints *simpliciter* – who are substantively what they are already in relation to him. The narrative of the Christian story which provides the contours for Christian living envisions a day when these several evaluations of our character meet, are reconciled, and no longer stand in tension. Until that day, however, we live within the constraints of a temporal narrative – adding virtues piecemeal, shaping being by doing, unable to see ourselves whole. And hence, until that day the virtue of hope must be the *leitmotif* of Christian existence, the fundamental shape of Christian character – hope that God can make of our piecemeal virtues more than we see or know and thus bring the plot of this story to a happy ending. The tensions involved in any attempt to think both ways about virtue – the tension between the self-mastery of moral virtue and a self perfectly passive before God; the tension between a virtue which we can claim as our possession, upon which we and others can rely, and a virtue which must be continually reestablished by divine grace; the tension between a self which can see itself only in part and a self whole before God – these are the tensions important for any theological analysis of virtue. We see them clearly in Luther's theology because they are so central to his concern, but they are crucial anytime we try to think theologically about virtue. The tensions are nicely captured by St. Paul in one short verse: "Not that I have already obtained this or am already perfect; but I press on to make it my own, because Christ Jesus has made me his own" (Philippians 3:12). Both ways of talking about virtue are necessary and will be necessary for as long as we remain pilgrims, caught up in a story which begins and ends in God but which moves toward its final curtain in the bit-by-bit medium of time and history.

Practical Difficulties of the Unexamined Life

Even if the discussion above helps locate the place of virtue in the Christian life, we need not deny that it may prove difficult to translate theory into practice and find a way to do justice to both senses of virtue in our lives. Since we have used Luther's writings as the prism through which to examine a theological understanding of virtue, we may use the movement which bears his name to illustrate this difficulty. In a fascinating book, *Luther's House of Learning*, Gerald Strauss has suggested that Lutheran attempts to indoctrinate the young were largely a failure.[11] The Lutherans were heirs of an educational tradition which held that, in the words of Plutarch, "moral virtue is habit long continued" (p. 63). They were heirs, that is, of a tradition which attempted to shape being by doing. Yet, no theme in Luther's theology had greater urgency than the belief that only God could finally transform the heart, transform character.

The difficulty faced by Protestant educators was, therefore, to "forge a motivational link" between the external discipline of habit and moral education and the inner spirit (p. 237). Committed to the view that virtues could be shaped by habit *and* to the view that true virtue was the work solely of divine grace – committed, that is, to the two understandings of virtue we have isolated in Luther's writings – these Protestant pedagogues labored to shape an educational practice which made place for both. The word *einbilden* became a key term in Protestant educational theory.

How could religious and moral precepts be imprinted so lastingly on men's hearts, minds, and characters as to redirect their impulses? Protestant theology and pedagogical practice clashed on the answer to this ques-

> tion. . . . All agreed that only God could turn the in-
> dividual's heart. . . . Nonetheless, Protestant educators
> proposed to bring about just such a fundamental change
> in men's natures. Luther himself pointed the way toward
> this transformation. The word of God, he suggested, can
> be impressed (*eingebildet*) upon the hearts of men to
> allow the divine spirit to do its work there. (p. 152)

A moment's consideration will suggest, of course, that this is more a statement than a resolution of the difficulty; for it leaves unexplained the link between strenuous education efforts to inculcate virtue and the claim that these efforts are entirely unable to bring about the fundamental transformation that is needed.

Strauss concludes that if the Reformation's purpose in Germany was "to make people – all people – think, feel, and act as Christians, to imbue them with a Christian mind-set, motivational drive, and way of life, it failed" (p. 307). And he explains this failure by suggesting that Lutheran educational efforts were hamstrung from the outset by ambivalence. "Torn between their trust in the molding power of education and their admission that the alteration of men's nature was a task beyond human strength, they strove for success in their endeavors while conceding the likelihood of defeat" (p. 300). The goal – true virtue – was so lofty that it could do little more than call into question the worth of the everyday methods of habituation to which they were also committed. Rather than finding some way of holding both senses of virtue in fruitful tension, they were paralyzed in their education efforts by their commitment to true virtue. Seeking the virtue which only God could work but mindful of its rarity, they committed themselves – but only halfheartedly – to the external disciplines of moral education.

> Lutherans seem to have lacked the temper, or the
> stomach, for such measures. They had opportunities for

creating social pressure, but they failed to turn them into a molding process. They insisted that everyone in society should be subjected to internal and external coercion, but they shunned police-state methods (for which they lacked the means, in any case) and treated with resigned tolerance the widespread deviation from their exalted norms. (p. 301)

Of course, the tension and ambivalence which Strauss detects are not a Lutheran problem alone, though it may be that—because Luther's theology focused so emphatically on character and the meaning of human righteousness—within Christian history the problem comes to its clearest expression in Lutheranism. The tension must always be present in Christian theory and practice, and theological analysis can sometimes do little more than unveil it. Christian character requires a kind of soulcraft, an ability to transform and reshape the person at his innermost core. And this, Christians believe, must be the prerogative of God alone; for he alone sees the self whole and entire. At the same time, Christians are committed to cultivation of the virtues, if only in piecemeal fashion. These virtues do at least foster human life together and fashion human behavior—if not character in the fullest sense—in a way which more closely approximates God's will for human life. We cultivate the virtues, knowing the dangers which always plague such efforts and aware that there is a certain futility in our attempts, since the tree determines the fruit.

The tension between these several views of virtue cannot, I think, be removed from the Christian perspective. Its theoretical resolution lies in the narrative Christians tell and retell—a story, not yet finished, in which God is graciously at work transforming sinners into saints. But that story, because it is not yet finished, must be lived. The theoretical resolution explains but does not remove the tensions of the practical life.

Within human history Christians are committed to the attempt to shape character by inculcating virtues. But they are committed also to the belief that this attempt is safe – protected to some extent against the moral paralysis which comes from focusing upon self, from our illusions of self-mastery and our tendency to claim virtue as our possession, from the temptation to step across the gap which divides inculcation of the virtues from shaping the soul – only when we do more than just attempt to transform being by doing. Our attempts at moral education are safe only when we also gather to worship, when we continually return to hear the Word which announces that the end of the story is present now in hope – the Word which makes present the grace of One who sees us whole and has both authority and power to transform character and shape souls. To tend the soul is a high calling. But it is done safely only by those who know the truth that the examined life is not worth living.[12]

6. It Killed the Cat

The Vice of Curiosity

Long ago there was a man of great intellect and great courage. He was a remarkable man, a giant, able to answer questions that no other human being could answer, willing boldly to face any challenge or problem. He was a confident man, a masterful man. He saved his city from disaster and ruled it as a father rules his children, revered by all. But something was wrong in his city. A plague had fallen on generation; infertility afflicted plants, animals, and human beings. The man confidently promised to uncover the cause of the plague and to cure the infertility. Resolutely, dauntlessly, he put his sharp mind to work to solve the problem, to bring the dark things to light. No secrets, no reticences, a full public inquiry. He raged against the representatives of caution, moderation, prudence, and piety, who urged him to curtail his inquiry; he accused them of trying to usurp his rightfully earned power, of trying to replace human and masterful control with submissive reverence. The story ends in tragedy: He solved the problem but, in making visible and public the dark and intimate details of his origins, he ruined his life, and that of his family. In the end, too late, he learns about the price of presumption, of overconfidence, of the overweening desire to master and control one's fate, In symbolic rejection of his desire to look into everything, he punishes his eyes with self-inflicted blindness.

Sophocles seems to suggest that such a man is always in principle – albeit unwillingly – a patricide, a regicide, and a practitioner of incest. We men of modern science may have something to learn from our forebear, Oedipus. It appears that Oedipus, being the kind of man an Oedipus is (the chorus calls him a paradigm of man), had no choice but to learn through suffering. Is it really true that we too have no other choice?[1]

Stop an average set of parents on the street, ask them whether they think it good to stimulate their children's curiosity, and an affirmative answer is almost a certainty. Curiosity in the young child is, we are assured, one of the signs of high intelligence. Our schools initiate special programs for "gifted children" (who turn out to be rather large in number) designed, among other things, to stimulate the curiosity of such children. The bits and pieces of psychology we all pick up suggest that human beings have a natural curiosity, that to inhibit it is to prevent our full development as persons, and even that much psychological illness comes from the attempt *not* to know certain truths about ourselves. Not to be curious turns out to be a sign of limited intelligence, moral weakness which fears responsibility, even illness.

One of the books I read to my children – not in an attempt to stimulate their curiosity but simply because I believe in sharing with them things I care about – has caused me to wonder whether curiosity is so unambiguously a good. In *The Magician's Nephew*[2] C. S. Lewis helps the child – and the adult – see that there may be something excessive, something morally troublesome, in a certain kind of curiosity.

Polly and Digory are curious children, curious about the empty house a little down the street. As a result they end up, not in that empty house, but in the study of Digory's Uncle Andrew. For years Uncle Andrew has been dabbling in magic, trying to discover the secret of the box of dust left him by his godmother, Mrs. Lefay. Just before her death, Uncle Andrew had promised that he would burn the box without opening it. That promise he did not keep for a reason he makes clear to Digory. "Men like me who possess hidden wisdom, are freed from common rules just as we are cut off from common pleasures. Ours, my boy, is a high and lonely destiny" (p. 16). After many years of study and much experimenting on guinea pigs – some of whom died, some of whom exploded, at least one of whom disappeared – Uncle Andrew succeeded in fashioning the dust into rings: yellow rings which would cause anyone touching them to vanish into another world; green rings to bring them back (or so Uncle Andrew hoped). Having tricked Polly into taking a yellow ring – and vanishing – Uncle Andrew then persuades Digory that it is his duty to go after her, carrying along a green ring by which they can both return.

Clearly, something has gone wrong with Uncle Andrew's curiosity. Indeed, later when he himself gets into the newly created world of Narnia, he is unable to marvel at the wonder of the world coming into existence. He becomes interested only when he discovers that a piece of scrap iron tossed into the fertile soil of Narnia might grow into a battleship. He sees nothing in Narnia except commercial possibilities (pp. 98f.).

Uncle Andrew's entire life has been dominated by a vice of curiosity, but others are also curious. Polly and Digory were curious about the empty house – and ended up in Uncle Andrew's study. Polly is curious about the yellow ring – and finds herself in another world. Digory, having followed her, is curious about other worlds and wants to explore rather than return immediately – and, as a result, they end up in the seemingly dead world of Charn. In the palace of Charn, where Digory and Polly see figures of former kings and queens now dead, they find "a little golden arch from which there hung a little golden bell; and beside this there lay a little golden hammer to hit the bell with" (p. 44). On the pillar holding arch and bell a short poetic stanza is cut in stone.

> Make your choice, adventurous Stranger;
> Strike the bell and bide the danger,
> Or wonder, till it drives you mad,
> What would have followed if you had. (p. 44)

Polly is at once ready to leave, but Digory cannot. Driven by the belief that he must know what he can know, he responds.

"Oh but don't you see it's no good!" said Digory. "We can't get out of it now. We shall always be wondering what would have happened if we had struck the bell. I'm not going home to be driven mad by always thinking of that. No fear!" (pp. 44f.)

This time the consequences of Digory's curiosity are more momentous. He strikes the bell, the world of Charn begins to crumble at the tone, and Jadis, last of the queens of Charn, comes to life. As they hurry with her to escape the falling ruins, Jadis tells Digory and Polly of Charn's last days. She and her sister had struggled over the kingdom. Both sides had promised not to use magic in the struggle. First Jadis's sister broke her promise – foolishly, since only Jadis knew "the secret of the Deplorable Word" (p. 54). Other rulers of Charn, while knowing that there was such a word which "if spoken with the proper ceremonies, would destroy all living things except the one who spoke it," had taken oaths not even to seek to know the word (p. 54). Jadis, however, had "learned it in a secret place and paid a terrible price to learn it" (p. 54). And having learned it, she used it. In the moment of her sister's seeming victory, she spoke the Deplorable Word – and Charn was no more.

The vice of curiosity – in Uncle Andrew, Digory and Polly, Jadis – exacts its price. Jadis – and with her evil – is brought to the new world of Narnia in the very moment of its creation. The toll falls heaviest, at least for a time, on Digory. When he realizes that Narnia is like a land of youth, Digory begins to hope for a chance to take back some of the fruit of Narnia to his mother, who is dying. Aslan, however, sends him on a journey. Digory is to go beyond the borders of Narnia, into the Western Wild, till he finds "a green valley with a blue lake in it, walled round by mountains of ice. At the end of the lake there is a steep, green hill. On the top of that hill there is a garden. In the centre of that garden is a tree. Pluck an apple from that tree and bring it back to me" (p. 128). From that apple will grow the Tree of Protection which will keep Narnia safe from Jadis for many a year.

Digory reaches the garden. Written on its gate is this stanza:

> Come in by the gold gates or not at all,
> Take of my fruit for others or forbear.
> For those who steal or those who climb my wall
> Shall find their heart's desire and find despair. (p. 141)

Digory enters (through the gates), picks an apple from the tree, and puts it in his pocket. Before putting it away, though, he cannot resist smelling it.

> It would have been better if he had not. A terrible thirst and hunger came over him and a longing to taste that fruit. He put it hastily into his pocket; but there were plenty of others. Could it be wrong to taste one? (p. 142)

Digory is saved from the temptation to take for himself—saved partly because he notices in the tree above a bird watching him, partly because the precept "Do Not Steal" had been hammered into his head as a boy.

He must yet face, however, a far more powerful temptation. Having resisted the desire to take for himself, he will now be tempted to take for others. Jadis has come to the garden ahead of Digory. He sees her now and turns to flee, but she stops him.

> "Foolish boy," said the Witch. "Why do you run from me? I mean you no harm. If you do not stop and listen to me now you will miss some knowledge that would have made you happy all your life." (p. 144)

Why, she asks, take back the apple of youth to the Lion Aslan? Why not eat it himself and live forever with her?

But that temptation – the appeal to Digory's curiosity and his desire for mastery – has already been overcome. Digory will not take for himself. Then Jadis cuts deeper. Why not take the apple for his mother?

> "Use your Magic and go back to your own world. A minute later you can be at your Mother's bedside, giving her the fruit. Five minutes later you will see the colour coming back to her face. She will tell you the pain is gone. Soon she will tell you she feels stronger. Then she will fall asleep – think of that; hours of sweet natural sleep, without pain, without drugs. Next day everyone will be saying how wonderfully she has recovered. Soon she will be quite well again. All will be well again. Your home will be happy again. You will be like other boys." (p. 145)

Why not indeed? The poem on the gates had, after all, said, "Take of my fruit for others or forbear." At the witch's suggestion, Digory gasps, realizing that "the most terrible choice lay before him" (p. 145). Aslan's instructions had been clear: to take one apple from the tree and return with it. Digory must now choose. He can obey those instructions or he can disobey in order to help his mother. He is strengthened to some extent in the face of this temptation by remembering once again the limits which the moral code imposes. He has made a promise to the Lion.

> "Mother herself," said Digory, getting the words out with difficulty, "wouldn't like it – awfully strict about keeping promises – and not stealing – and all that sort of thing. *She'd* tell me not to do it – quick as anything – if she was here." (p. 146)

Jadis suggests that no one need ever know what Digory has done, since he can leave Polly behind in Narnia. And suddenly Digory realizes that Jadis cares for him and his mother no more than she cares for Polly. She cares only that he join her in vice, that as her own curiosity has impelled her to eat the fruit of that tree, so should he. Realizing that, Digory returns at once and hears Aslan's "Well Done."

Later, when the apple has been planted and the Tree of Protection grown at once into a towering tree, Aslan gives Digory an apple from it to take to his mother. And Aslan explains that the tree will keep Jadis away from Narnia, since, having eaten its fruit in the wrong way and at the wrong time, she will forever loathe the fruit. Yet, the magic in the fruit will work. She has, as the poem on the gate of the garden warned, found her heart's desire and found despair.

> "She has won her heart's desire; she has unwearying strength and endless days like a goddess. But length of days with an evil heart is only length of misery and already she begins to know it. All get what they want: they do not always like it." (p. 157)

Aslan also explains that had Digory stolen an apple it would have healed his mother, but it would not have brought joy. "The day would have come when both you and she would have looked back and said it would have been better to die in that illness" (p. 158).

An adult reading *The Magician's Nephew* can hardly fail to note that curiosity is, in this story, a vice. And we may hope that children also absorb this insight as they absorb so much else from the stories they hear and read. Nevertheless, it is just as clear that we do not learn from *The Magician's Nephew* that the pursuit of knowledge is itself bad. Readers of this story, and of *The Lion, The Witch, and the Wardrobe*, will know that Digory grew up to become Professor Kirke—a man not only learned but wise. If curiosity is a vice, therefore, it cannot be equated simply with the desire to know. The story sometimes suggests that curiosity is vicious when it involves the pursuit of useless knowledge—but more often that the vice of curiosity involves a search for power and control, a thirst that *must* be filled, a pursuit not limited by the claims of morality.

That curiosity may be a vice is no new discovery in Christian thought. In the sections that follow we will explore briefly what three great Christian thinkers—St. Augustine, St. Thomas Aquinas, and John Henry Newman—have to teach us about curiosity. None is likely to be as unambiguously positive as our average modern parent, and in attending to these thinkers we may learn better what curiosity to stimulate in our children and what curiosity may kill, not only the cat, but us and our children as well.

Augustine: The Lust of the Eyes

In Book X of his *Confessions*³ Augustine, having charted the course by which he was drawn to faith, takes stock of his present condition. He considers that he must confess not only his past but also his present; for the journey toward virtue never ends in this life, and only God can see us whole and entire. To that end he discusses some of the temptations to which a Christian is subject, considering the degree to which he is successful in his own struggle against them. Many of these temptations he includes within the threefold biblical rubric, "the lust of the flesh and the lust of the eyes and the pride of life" (I John 2:16).

He discusses first the lusts of the flesh, considering the pleasures made possible by our bodily senses. Thus, he discusses the proper use of food and music, hewing always to the line that the pleasures themselves are good, but we are not when we fail to refer them back to the God who gives them. The same is true, it turns out, of the desire for knowledge; for Augustine then turns in X, 35 to the "lust of the eyes," which here means not one of the temptations given in bodily sensation but the temptation which comes from the desire to see, to know.

The lust of the eyes is, Augustine writes, "in many ways more dangerous" than the lust of the flesh. This vice, "dignified by the names of learning and science" is "a kind of empty longing and curiosity which aims not at taking pleasure in the flesh but at acquiring experience through the flesh." We note that Augustine does *not* write that all learning and science are merely vice; he says that sometimes we practice vice and dignify it with the honorable names of learning and science. This vice of curiosity, which Augustine terms the lust of eyes, is quite different from our more ordinary search for pleasures through the lust of the flesh. Augustine notes perceptively that curiosity, our desire to *see*, may lead us to seek what is not in the ordinary sense pleasurable at all. Like Uncle Andrew studying the secret of the magic dust, or Jadis trying to learn the Deplorable Word, we may expend life and energy, we may suffer greatly, "simply because of the lust to find out and know." Curiosity may move us to seek, not what is beautiful, sweet, or harmonious, but the opposite of these. We may, Augustine writes, chancing upon a strikingly contemporary example, rush to see a "mangled corpse," though there is certainly no pleasure in the sight. It arouses in us horror; yet we desire to see.

Some of Augustine's other examples may strike us as trivial. Can it be vice if, while walking through the country, Augustine finds himself stopping out of curiosity to watch a dog coursing a hare? Or catches himself idly observing a spider entangling flies in its web? Or even, can it be serious vice when we listen to gossip out of curiosity and are drawn to take a serious interest in it? We may have difficulty imagining that any of these can involve serious vice. But, of course, a temptation immediately seen as temptation is no temptation at all. Hence, Screwtape's advice to Wormwood:

You will say that these are very small sins; and doubtless, like all young tempters, you are anxious to be able to report spectacular wickedness. But do remember, the only thing that matters is the extent to which you separate the man from the Enemy. It does not matter how small the sins are, provided that their cumulative effect is to edge the man away from the Light and out into the Nothing. Murder is no better than cards if cards can do the trick. Indeed, the safest road to Hell is the gradual one – the gentle slope, soft underfoot, without sudden turnings, without milestones, without signposts.[4]

When we focus on that aspect of morality which evaluates our deeds and their effects for good or ill upon our neighbors, we are certainly entitled to view with relative equanimity that curiosity which stops to watch the hounds chasing hares. But when we consider traits of character and the development in us of both virtue and vice, what is for the moment insignificant from the point of view of the neighbor may nevertheless be all-important. It is, therefore, worth taking Augustine seriously and asking what he thinks is vice in curiosity.

Some of his examples suggest that curiosity might simply be a desire to know what is useless. He writes: "From the same motive [curiosity] men proceed to investigate the workings of nature which is beyond our ken – things which it does no good to know and which men only want to know for the sake of knowing." An antiquated view, we are likely to respond, which had it triumphed would have left us without the benefits of modern science. But there is a little more than this to Augustine's understanding of curiosity. The same Augusine who can write here in his *Confessions*, "I am not interested in knowing about the courses of the stars," could also years later write the following striking paragraph in his *City of God*:

Who can adequately describe, or even imagine, the work of the Almighty? . . . There are all the important arts discovered and developed by human genius, some for necessary uses, others simply for pleasure. Man shows remarkable powers of mind and reason in the satisfaction of his aims, even though they may be unnecessary, or even dangerous and harmful; and those powers are evidence of the blessings he enjoys in his natural powers which enable him to discover, to learn, and to practise those arts. Think of the wonderful inventions of clothing and building, the astounding achievements of human industry! Think of man's progress in agriculture and navigation; of the variety, in conception and accomplishment, man has shown in pottery, in sculpture, in painting; the marvels in theatrical spectacles, in which man's contrivances in design and production have excited wonder in the spectators and incredulity in the minds of those who heard of them; all his ingenious devices for the capturing, killing, or taming of wild animals. Then there are all the weapons against his fellow-man in the shape of prisons, arms, and engines of war; all the medical resources for preserving or restoring health; all the seasonings or spices to gratify his palate or to tickle his appetite. Consider the multitudinous variety of the means of information and persuasion, among which the spoken and written word has the first place; the enjoyment afforded to the mind by the trappings of eloquence and the rich diversity of poetry; the delight given to the ears by the instruments of music and the melodies of all kinds that man has discovered. Consider man's skill in geometry and arithmetic, his intelligence shown in plotting the positions and courses of the stars. How abundant is man's stock of knowledge of natural phenomena! It is beyond description, especially if one should choose to dwell upon particulars, instead of heaping all together in a general mass. Finally, the brilliant wit shown by philosophers and heretics in defending their very errors and falsehoods is something which beggars imagination![5]

The man who could write these lines and marvel at the discoveries of the human mind – "some for necessary uses, others simply for pleasure" – appreciated the dangers involved in our desire to know but was not likely to rest content in a characterization of curiosity as a search for useless knowledge. It is important to note that in the sentences which follow immediately his criticism of our desire to know "things which it does no good to know" Augustine mentions magic and the desire even of religious believers to have signs and portents from God, "simply for the experience of seeing them."

We come closer to Augustine's central concern when we note that he describes curiosity as "the empty desire to possess." What is crucial is not so much what is known as how and why we seek to know. Robert Meagher has pointed to a central Augustinian distinction between what Meagher calls the "life of wisdom" and the "life of power."[6] For a human being to achieve happiness, Augustine believed, two things were necessary: (1) the wisdom to will what is good, and (2) the power to possess what one wills. The misery of human life, for Augustine, was that we are forced to choose between these two requirements; we cannot have both. We must either (1) will what is good, but not possess it, or (2) possess what we will, but not will what is good.

> What clearly follows from these two alternatives is an altogether Augustinian distinction between two fundamental possibilities available to human being; we may call them the life of wisdom and the life of power. . . .
> It seems that one may either strive to want the right thing, or strive to have what one wants. The search for wisdom somehow involves the renunciation of power, the renunciation of possession, while the search for power somehow involves the renunciation of wisdom,

since it presupposes the appropriateness of what it is striving to attain. . . . Each of these two lives has its own peculiar threat or risk. The life of wisdom is threatened by final resourcelessness, by the possibility that in the end one will possess no more than one does in the course of one's life. The life of power, on the other hand, is threatened by final foolishness, by the possibility that in the end one will find one's attainment futile or even bitter.

This context helps us to understand Augustine's characterization of that curiosity which is vice as "the empty desire to possess." He means, I think, that sometimes our desire to know is only a greedy longing for a new kind of experience: We seek not simply increased understanding of the creation; we want the thrill of seeing, the experience of knowing. This empty desire to possess is vice. And it is, we can now see, something quite different from a desire for "useless" knowledge. We may want to know what seems useless but want thereby simply increased understanding of the creation *given* us, a creation we neither possess nor control. We may, on the other hand, seek to know something of benefit to many others; yet we may be moved not by thought of their benefit but by our desire to *see*. The "empty desire to possess" which Augustine regards as vice cannot co-exist with an appreciation of the world as given us, as placed into our care. If our world has been given us, even our quest to know is limited by the Giver – it is a search for understanding, not for power or esoteric experience. Hence, what is crucial for Augustine is not the substance of the knowledge we seek but the motive which stirs the intellect. There are substantive limits, of course, but only because a desire to know certain things is incompatible with the receptive spirit which accepts the world from God and finds its limit in God. Hard as it may be to state the limits precisely, it is the part of virtue to recognize those times when we must not gratify our desire to know.

Many possibilities may pique my curiosity – I may wonder how my neighbor's wife performs in bed; how human beings respond to experiments harmful to their bodies, or even to suffering; how the development of a fertilized egg could be stimulated to produce a monster rather than a normal human being; how to preserve a human being alive forever. I may wonder, but it would be wrong to seek to know.[7] Not, in every case, because I cannot know, but because I cannot possess such knowledge while willing what is good. To accept such limits is, of course, to face what Meagher terms the threat of "final resourcelessness," but that is the risk Augustine would have us run. To love the good and to possess what we love are, in this life, not always compatible. Hence, to seek always to love the good is to commit ourselves to a life that seeks to receive, not to possess.

Although Augustine does not outline for us any general principle by which we can always distinguish a proper desire for knowledge from the vice of curiosity, we can learn from him the attitude which may at least make virtue possible – an attitude characterized by a reverent desire to understand creation rather than a longing to possess the experience of knowing. Such a life may be threatened by final resourcelessness. That should be no surprise; for those who have pondered the meaning of virtue and vice have always returned to the question, "Can a good man be harmed?" Virtue itself can offer no guarantees that all endings will be as happy as Digory's. But this much must be certain for anyone who has been instructed by Augustine: Curiosity, indulged without a sense of limits, must be vice in us and must lead to that final foolishness in which we possess what we love – and find that it does not satisfy.

Aquinas: *Studiositas* and *Curiositas*

It did not require the insights of modern psychology to discover that in the human being "there is a natural urge to find out. . . ." These are the words of St. Thomas Aquinas (S.T., 2a2ae, q. 166, a. 2).[8] Having said that, however, Aquinas goes on to remark that this natural urge needs to be guided, as do all human desires and appetites. Sometimes our sluggishness inclines us to suppress this urge and shirk the hard work that "finding out" involves; therefore, we need the virtue of *studiositas*, a disposition to be diligent in the pursuit of knowledge (and the topic discussed in 2a2ae, q. 166). At other times our desire to know may be excessive in certain ways; then we fall prey to the vice of *curiositas* (discussed in 2a2ae, q. 167). Thus, Aquinas is clear from the outset that the natural urge to know is not simply to be suppressed; instead, in this as in all things we are to be temperate.

Even to moderate our appetite for knowledge, to think of curiosity as a vice, may seem something of an embarrassment to us. Indeed, the editor of the volume in which the questions treating *curiositas* and *studiositas* appear seems to feel keenly this possibility. He therefore provides us with two footnotes designed to alleviate the embarrassment by providing historical context. At the beginning of q. 166 a footnote points out that while *docilitas* (teachableness) had long been honored in Christian thought,

> less prominent was the zest for scientific discovery which grew with the 13th century and was so energetically exemplified in St. Albert the Great, the teacher of St. Thomas. If this Question can be taken as a tribute to the Albertine school, the next Question, on the deviation-form, curiosity, can appear as a sop to its

critics – and these were, and still are, many among the devout.[9]

Again, at q. 167, a. 1, a similar footnote is offered.

> The discussion is conducted, possibly with more embarrassment than the author betrays, against a background of hostility to "profane" science present in a vigorous theological tradition, and expressed even by the early Dominican masters and in Order legislation. Defeated by the weight of the High Scholastics, notably Albert, it represents a perennial protest, and the *scientia inflat* line was a major theme in the criticism of the schoolmen by the *theologia moderna* of the 14th century and afterwards.[10]

One wonders, however, whether St. Thomas might betray little embarrassment because he felt little. He considers precisely the objection that since knowledge in itself is a good, no vice of curiosity could enter into our intellectual knowing, which would be good *simpliciter*; and to this objection he responds as follows:

> The good for man lies in knowing the truth, and his sovereign good lies, not in knowing any sort of truth, but in the perfect knowledge of the supreme truth, as Aristotle shows. So therefore there can be a vice in knowing some truth inasmuch as the desire at work is not duly ordered to the knowledge of the supreme truth in which the highest felicity consists. (2a2ae, q. 167, a. 1, ad. 2)

The language is not Augustine's, but the sentiment is similar. For what is Aquinas saying if not that in order to will what is supremely good we may on some occasions have to curb our appetite for knowledge? He as much as Augustine is ready to accept the limit placed upon our natural urge to know by the truth that living rightly and possessing what we desire are not always compatible. Hence, Josef Pieper can explicate the vice of *curiositas* as enjoying the act of seeing itself, seeking to possess what we love.

> There is a gratification in seeing that reverses the original meaning of vision and works disorder in man himself. The true meaning of seeing is perception of reality. But "concupiscence of the eyes" does not aim to perceive reality, but to enjoy "seeing."[11]

In his discussion Aquinas suggests several ways in which our natural appetite for knowledge can be corrupted by the vice of curiosity. It may—a very ordinary sort of corruption, as when Augustine stopped to watch the hounds—lead us to idle away time that ought to be devoted to the duties of our office. We may in our curiosity seek knowledge from an illicit source; Aquinas's illustration is having recourse to evil spirits, but we could no doubt think of other illegitimate means by which we today seek knowledge. We may, Aquinas suggests, try to know the "truth about creatures" but ignore the fact that the proper end of the creature is God. And, of course, ignoring that end we may fail to set limits to our appetite for knowing. Our curiosity may be "directed to something noxious"—that is, toward an act unjust to others or evil in itself. We may wonder, for example, whether many of the movies watched today do not stimulate in us a desire to know what we ought not, whether many things read do not arouse is us a curiosity to know the rightful secrets of others. At the very least, we may agree with David Smith in his suggestion that knowledge may be untimely.

> My children must learn about sexual perversion, but it is not obvious that it is good for them to acquire this knowledge in the primary grades. *Perhaps* a person should always be told about the infidelity of a spouse, but there are certainly better and worse times and ways to

communicate that information. And the same thing applies to *scientific* truth.[12]

Our desire for knowledge, natural and praiseworthy as it is in itself, is only the raw material out of which we construct character, develop virtues and vices. We can learn – without embarrassment – from St. Thomas that we will develop not virtue but vice unless we remember that our appetite for knowledge must always remain appropriate to those who are creatures. It must be set within limits and governed by the understanding that we seek not simply the enjoyment of seeing but the truth of reality. And a part of that truth is Augustine's alternative: to will what is good *or* to possess what we will.

Newman: The Need for Elbowroom

In Augustine we found a thinker almost inclined to suggest that any hankering after useless knowledge amounted to a vice of curiosity. This is not, as we saw, Augustine's considered view; yet a part of him is drawn in that direction. In Aquinas we found a thinker who concurred in the limits Augustine placed on the desire for knowledge but without any of the hesitation to affirm and approve the natural human appetite for "finding out." When now we turn to John Henry Newman's *The Idea of a University*[13] we find a thinker who does not hesitate to say what most of us, almost by conditioned reflex, believe: that "any kind of knowledge, if it be really such, is its own reward" and that knowledge is "its own end" (p. 77). In the domain not of faith but of thought, Newman writes, "Great minds need elbowroom. . . . And so indeed do lesser minds, and all minds" (p. 358). Here at last is one who seems to speak our language and sympathize with our concerns. It will be instructive to discover, therefore, whether Newman sets any limits to the quest of the restless, searching intellect. (It is clear, of course, that he does set such limits in the realm of dogma, where he believes the Church must be recognized as an authoritative teacher. But we will for the most part concern ourselves with the more general search for wisdom of any kind.)

We note first how strongly Newman emphasizes that we cannot ask of the quest for knowledge that it develop virtue in the soul. If knowledge need not always be directed toward some useful, practical end, neither must it seek "to steel the soul against temptation or to console it in affliction." The search for knowledge needs no justification beyond itself, and Newman will offer none. "Knowledge is one thing, virtue is another; good sense is not conscience, refinement is not humility, nor is largeness and justness of view faith. . . . Liberal education makes not the Christian, not the Catholic, but the gentleman" (p. 91). Newman's purpose in emphasizing this point in Discourse V (titled, "Knowledge Its Own End") is chiefly to make clear, against all those who would require of liberal education some practical purpose, that human beings rightly seek to know simply for the sake of knowing. But he is also concerned lest we should imagine that intellectual refinement is any guarantee of moral virtue. "Quarry the granite rock with razors, or moor the vessel with a thread of silk; then may you hope with such keen and delicate instruments as human knowledge and human reason to contend against those giants, the passion and the pride of man" (p. 91).

It may well be that Newman digs the chasm too deep between intellectual and moral virtue. Seeing the truth may require that we discipline the fat relentless ego, and this may be inseparable from the moral discipline required to accept the just claims of others when they conflict with our own. Thus, it may be that "seeing" reality requires in the end not only intellectual curiosity and discipline but the moral virtues which help us to be honest, just, and temperate. Whatever we decide on this point, it is evident that Newman wishes to separate, at least in thought, the quest for knowledge and moral virtue. Each is a good appropriate to the human being. Each is therefore to be affirmed. As there is in moral virtue "a beauty of our moral being," so "in like manner there is a beauty, there is a perfection of the intellect."

> To open the mind, to correct it, to refine it, to enable it to know, and to digest, master, rule, and use its knowledge, to give it power over its own faculties, application, flexibility, method, critical exactness, sagacity, resource, address, eloquent expression, is an object as intelligible . . . as the cultivation of virtue, while, at the same time, it is absolutely distinct from it. (pp. 92-93)

What Newman does not here tell us is how these two goods for the human being are to be weighed. He is concerned to make the case for freedom for the restless, searching mind. But he never hints that he regards this as the highest of goods. Indeed, his language suggests something quite different. Intellectual curiosity, discovery, and investigation – intellectual refinement as liberal education develops it – all this is for Newman one of the human goods. But like all such goods it must be placed into the service of that which is higher. The passion to know is praiseworthy in a human being; so are many other aims. Hence, "as a hospital or an almshouse, though its end be ephemeral, may be sanctified to the service of religion, so surely may a university. . . . We perfect our nature, not by undoing it, but by adding to it what is more than nature, and directing it towards aims higher than its own" (p. 93).

Newman's strong affirmation of the intellect and its powers is not taken back but is qualified when viewed in the light of the final end of human life – what in Newman's language is "more than nature." Once again, therefore, as with Augustine and Aquinas, the affirmation of the urge to know is an affirmation of a *creaturely* urge. The desire for knowledge cannot be healthy if separated from this larger context. Newman's language, as we have cited it thus far, would suggest, however, two rather separate spheres, each intact by itself, but needing to be brought together in a relation of lower and higher stages of development of character. His language suggests that intellectual cultivation can be satisfactorily pursued on its own, but that for the completion of human character we must add to such cultivation a certain moral and religious aim. As we probe more deeply into Newman's idea of education we find, however, that these two spheres do not – and cannot – remain separate. It turns out that, from the very beginning, intellectual cultivation can only attain its aim if it is guided and permeated by a religious spirit.

This becomes evident in Discourse VIII, in which Newman treats "Knowledge Viewed in Relation to Religious Duty." He begins by arguing that the search for knowledge, even if it does not directly serve religion, tends to draw the mind toward subjects "worthy a rational being" and in that sense works something good. Yet, he must immediately admit that "this mental cultivation, even when it is successful for the purpose for which I am applying it, may be from the first nothing more than the substitution of pride for sensuality" (p. 141). And indeed, this turns out to be one of the themes of Discourse VIII. "The radical difference indeed of this mental refinement from genuine religion, in spite of its seeming relationship, is the very cardinal point on which my present discussion turns" – and the reader may be a little surprised to be told now that this is the "cardinal point" of Newman's discussion (pp. 144-145). Newman goes on to note the difference between a conscience which, though sensitive and cultivated, regards duty as "a sort of taste" and sin as an offense against our human nature rather than against God – the difference between such a conscience which has become "a mere self-respect" and the genuinely religious conscience (pp. 145-146). He contrasts the civilized virtue of modesty with the Christian virtue of humility and notes of modesty that "so little is it the necessary index of humility that it is even compatible with pride" (p. 157). The modest control of "outward deportment" was possible for the cultivated gentleman of Newman's day, but enlargement of the intellect could not by itself make possible that radical transformation of character which is humility. Under the guise of modesty, pride still asserts itself as self-respect; as such, Newman writes, "it is the very household god of society" (p. 158).

Here, then, we see Newman stressing not two separate spheres, each good in itself, but a oneness of character and the sense in which all virtues interpenetrate. "The world is content with setting right the surface of things; the Church aims at regenerating the very depths of the heart" (p. 154). Such a regenerating is not likely to leave even our seeming virtues – even the acknowledged goods of intellectual curiosity and refinement – untouched or untransformed. Newman's argument in Discourse VIII culminates in his justly famous definition of a gentleman, too long to quote and too majestic to summarize or abbreviate. Having sketched in words what a gentleman is, Newman writes:

> Such are some of the lineaments of the ethical character which the cultivated intellect will form, apart from religious principle. They are seen within the pale of the Church and without it, in holy men, and in profligate; they form the *beau ideal* of the world; they partly assist and partly distort the development of the Catholic. (pp. 160-161)

Here for a moment the two spheres reassert themselves and the claims of the intellect and its development seem separate from religious limits or direction. The character of the gentleman, as it is "apart from religious principle" can "partly assist . . . the development of the Catholic." But it can also "partly distort" such development, and Newman's closing sentence – contrasting the great Christian Father Basil and the apostate Emperor Julian – reasserts once again the belief that no part of human character, including our desire to know, can be safely cultivated except as the virtue of a creature directed toward and limited by God: "Basil and Julian were fellow students at the schools of Athens; and one became the saint and doctor of the Church, the other her scoffing and relentless foe" (p. 161).

In Newman we find a great willingness – even eagerness – to affirm the natural urge to know. But we find also the clear conviction that intellectual curiosity and refinement, though a good for human beings, is not the only such good nor the highest. As a result Newman is driven to suggest, almost against his will, that the passion to know cannot be fully good and healthy if separated from the love for God which limits and transforms it. Isolated from that context, any affirmation of intellect and reason must become that "religion of reason" which Newman depicts so powerfully in the character of the Emperor Julian. He describes him as "all but the pattern-man of philosophical virtue" and as "one of the most eminent specimens of pagan virtue" (pp. 147-148). Yet, in him finally "we recognize the mere philosopher" (p. 149). Even his virtue – though called that – must be judged shallow, meager, and unamiable "when brought upon its critical trial by his sudden summons into the presence of his Judge" (p. 148). The urge to know, if we are to transmute it into the stuff of virtue, must remain a creaturely urge. Our search for knowledge must accept limits or become an empty and destructive urge to possess. This much is affirmed also by Newman, who believed so strongly that all minds need elbowroom.

The Vice of Curiosity

To be curious is not simply to hanker after useless knowledge, but it is true that curiosity may often lead us into explorations and investigations which appear unlikely to benefit anyone in particular. Nothing I have drawn from the writings of Augustine, Aquinas, or Newman suggests that such curiosity is always vice. It becomes vice only when we set no limits to our curiosity, when we can never find reasons why we *ought* not gratify our desire to see and know, when we regard no secrets as closed to our inquiring minds, when curiosity is bounded neither by respect for others nor reverence for God.

Sometimes, of course, our investigations and explorations are motivated not so much by curiosity as by the need to help someone. The researcher who is moved by curiosity to see what happens when sperm fertilizes ovum in a laboratory is not in precisely the same position as the researcher who investigates the same process because he hopes to help an infertile couple have children of "their own." Often of course – perhaps almost always – such research will be driven by both motivations. And each requires moral evaluation. Neither is, in itself and apart from further argument, sufficient justification. That we seek knowledge which will benefit others does not mean our search should recognize no limits. In such a case the end – benefit to others – is certainly worthy and justifies some means, but it will not justify *any* means. But I have not here been concerned with that kind of desire for knowledge. Instead, I have tried to pay attention to the appetite for knowledge which we often term curiosity and which seeks no end beyond the knowledge itself. The search is its own warrant, a search natural, compelling, and fulfilling for human beings; yet here also the appetite is not, in itself and without further argument, always sufficient justification. Such curiosity, when it becomes "the empty desire to possess" rather than to receive, when it seeks simply the enjoyment of seeing rather than understanding of created reality, has been thought by Christians to be vice. To be curious about the *creation* is to desire knowledge about a world which comes from One whose being and will limit us. An appetite for knowledge which lacks that vision of the world as creation is in peril of becoming the vice of curiosity. We cannot specify in detail the limits which must always circumscribe our urge to know. Perhaps we should not even attempt such specification; the path of virtue is not laid out in advance. But when the desire to know becomes a desire to control more than to receive, a thirst which must be satisfied, when it tempts us to transgress the limits and demands of ordinary morality – then we may be sure that the vice of curiosity lies near at hand.

To remember that curiosity killed the cat is to remember that the appetite for knowledge is not virtue but the raw material out of which we make either virtue or vice – and that vice is always destructive. If nothing else, it leads to that blindness which is self-inflicted; for if we do not see the world as the creation given to us, we do not, finally, see. This is simply one more instance of a fundamental truth of the moral life: to seek to master and to possess as our own whatever we love, even so certain a good as knowledge, is a sure sign that we do not love rightly. The end must be that having eyes, we do not see. Such blindness can perhaps be controlled by the disciplined cultivation of moral virtue, but its cure may require a remedy greater than virtue itself can offer.[14]

7: The Virtue of Gratitude

Then Peter came up and said to him, "Lord, how often shall my brother sin against me, and I forgive him? As many as seven times?" Jesus said to him, "I do not say to you seven times, but seventy times seven. Therefore the kingdom of heaven may be compared to a king who wished to settle accounts with his servants. When he began the reckoning, one was brought to him who owed him ten thousand talents; and as he could not pay, his lord ordered him to be sold, with his wife and children and all that he had, and payment to be made. So the servant fell on his knees, imploring him, 'Lord, have patience with me, and I will pay you everything.' And out of pity for him the lord of that servant released him and forgave him the debt. But that same servant as he went out, came upon one of his fellow servants who owed him a hundred denarii; and seizing him by the throat he said, 'Pay what you owe.' So his fellow servant fell down and besought him, 'Have patience with me, and I will pay you.' He refused and went and put him in prison till he should pay the debt. When his fellow servants saw what had taken place, they were greatly distressed, and they went and reported to their lord all that had taken place. Then his lord summoned him and said to him, 'You wicked servant! I forgave you all that debt because you besought me; and should not you have had mercy on your fellow servant, as I had mercy on you?' And in anger his lord delivered him to the jailers, till he should pay all his debt. So also my heavenly Father will do to every one of you, if you do not forgive your brother from your heart." (Matt. 18:21-35)

Prologue: A Meditation on Matthew 18:21–35

How can we be happy with the way this story ends? The servant is thrown into jail with very little chance of getting out again, and Jesus says, "So also my heavenly Father will do to every one of you, if you do not forgive your brother from your heart." This is a story about forgiveness, but there doesn't seem to be much of it for that unforgiving servant, or for us when we are like him. The context – in which Jesus tells Peter that we should forgive seventy times seven – leads us to expect a parable which will teach that forgiveness is always available, without limit. But the parable seems to say something quite different. The master hands the ungrateful servant over to the torturers, there to stay until he pays back his entire debt.

And that means forever. No bankruptcy laws in those days. No keeping your house and television set. For the person imprisoned for his debts there was little way out, little hope for release. What, we may well ask, has happened to unlimited forgiveness? Jesus requires it of his disciples. But the master in this story certainly doesn't show forgiveness without limit to the ungrateful servant – and the master is, Jesus says, like the heavenly Father.

We should notice that the point of this story is not unusual in the Bible. Every time we pray the Lord's Prayer we say, "forgive us our trespasses, as we forgive those who trespass against us." "As you sow, so shall you reap," the Scriptures say. The point is quite simple: There is something hypocritical about claiming that we want to live from the gifts and beneficence of God but being unwilling to give to others as we have received.

If we say that *we* live not by our merits but by the free gift of God and then demand that *others* get only what they deserve, our talk is suspect. If we care about gifts only when they benefit us, it begins to look as if what we care about is just our own skins. When that servant who had been forgiven so large a debt ran into his fellow servant who owed him a little, what he ran into was a test of how much he really believed in living by grace. And he failed the test. He didn't really like gifts. He simply believed in living by whatever principle was to his advantage at the moment.

As you sow, so shall you reap. We all finally decide by what law we wish to live – and then, willy-nilly, like it or not, we have to end up living by it. If with our families, friends, and acquaintances we determine to live by the rule of forgiveness, then that same forgiveness will be there for us when we need it most. If we live by the law of strict justice, then justice is what we will get, even when it hurts.

The gifts of God are always available. His grace knows no limit. But this God, when he gives freely, says: "freely you have received, freely give." Not everyone wants to be around a Lord like that. Not everyone wants to be grateful. The unforgiving servant was happy enough to be around the master when he was forgiven his debt. He didn't really want to be around him all the time, though; for he didn't want to live an entire life shaped by the pattern of gift and gratitude. This is the way of life in God's kingdom, its rule of existence: freely you have received, freely give. That servant liked the free receiving, but not the free giving. Which meant: he didn't really want to live in that kingdom. Maybe there wasn't much the master could do for him.

"All this he does out of his pure, fatherly, and divine goodness and mercy, without any merit or worthiness on my part. For all of this I am bound to thank, praise, serve, and obey him." It has been a good many years now since I first memorized those words from Luther's explanation in his Small Catechism of the first article of the Apostles' Creed. Since then I'm sure I have read these words more times than I could easily remember or number. I have taken them for granted, and yet they puzzle me. Perhaps they puzzle you too.

Let me add three more, similar, passages from Luther's Large Catechism to this one. Taken together they may help to explain my puzzlement.

Hence, since everything we possess, and everything in heaven and on earth besides, is daily given and sustained by God, it inevitably follows that we are in duty bound to love, praise, and thank him without ceasing, and, in short, to devote all these good things to his service . . . . [1]

He gives us all these things so that we may sense and see in them his fatherly heart and his boundless love toward us. Thus our hearts will be warmed and kindled with gratitude to God and a desire to use all these blessings to his glory and praise.[2]

Such, very briefly, is the meaning of this article. It is all that ordinary people need to learn at first, both about what we have and receive from God and about what we owe him in return.[3]

These passages puzzle me because of the relation — or relations — which they suggest between gift and gratitude. In several of the passages Luther suggests that a gift *obligates* us, that God's blessings create duties on our part, that we owe him gratitude in return for the gifts he showers upon us. Our own experience with gifts, both giving and receiving them, may suggest however that a gift which *requires* gratitude in return falls short of being a gift in the fullest sense. And indeed, in at least one of the passages I cited, Luther himself appears to shift ground somewhat. He uses a language other than the language of obligation. When we see God's gifts to us, he writes, "our hearts will be warmed and kindled with gratitude to God and a desire to use all these blessings to his glory and praise." Gift and gratitude are still connected here, but the connecting link is not that of duty and obligation but, instead, love and affection. In this passage the gift does not so much obligate us to be grateful as it elicits in us a desire to show gratitude. Luther seems to sense little tension between these formulations; yet they are not the same. It is these several ways of relating gift and gratitude in the Christian life which puzzle me. And this puzzlement is, I think, not simply an insignificant piece of my autobiography. Luther here formulates, in the context of an explanation of the first article of the creed, one of the basic themes of the Christian life. Gratitude to God for life itself and for the blessings enjoyed in life – gratitude to others for their gifts – is a fundamental Christian virtue, a basic characteristic of Christian existence. We seek therefore more than an end to some minor bewilderment which has come upon me while looking at the book shelves in my office. We want to know something important about the gratitude which characterizes – or, should we say, *ought* to characterize – our lives as Christians.

Gratitude Is an Obligation

The greatest portion of this chapter will be devoted to an effort to understand how gratitude is not simply an obligation for the Christian but is a virtue, a characteristic which molds and shapes our entire life. However, precisely because that is our goal and direction, it is essential that, at the outset, we say a good word for gratitude as a duty. Better obligatory gratitude, after all, than ingratitude.

And that is precisely the point. Sometimes these are our alternatives: an obligatory grateful act carried out even when we don't feel like it, or no show of gratitude at all. We can learn from the devilish advice Screwtape gives Wormwood in C. S. Lewis' *The Screwtape Letters*.[4] In trying to help Wormwood, a junior tempter, achieve some success in tempting his "patient," Screwtape describes the "law of undulation" – which, he says, Wormwood should have learned in Training College. This law is based on the fact that human beings are both animal and spiritual.

As spirits they belong to the eternal world, but as animals they inhabit time. This means that while their spirit can be directed to an eternal object, their bodies, passions, and imaginations are in continual change, for to be in time means to change. Their nearest approach to constancy, therefore, is undulation – the repeated return to a level from which they repeatedly fall back, a series of troughs and peaks. . . . The dryness and dullness through which your patient is now going are not, as you fondly suppose, your workmanship; they are merely a natural phenomenon which will do us no good unless you make a good use of it.

Screwtape goes on to enunciate a truth about "the Enemy": "He cannot ravish. He can only woo." That is, he will not coerce gratitude from unwilling people; he desires that it be freely offered. Therefore, he must leave his creatures free – even if that makes them susceptible to Wormwood's blandishments.

He leaves the creature free to stand on its own legs – to carry out from the will alone duties which have lost all relish. It is during such trough periods, much more than during the peak periods, that it is growing into the sort of creature He wants it to be. Hence the prayers offered in the state of dryness are those which please Him best . . . . He wants them to learn to walk and must therefore take away His hand; and if only the will to walk is really there He is pleased even with their stumbles. Do not be deceived, Wormwood. Our cause is never more in danger than when a human, no longer desiring, but still intending, to do our Enemy's will, looks round upon a universe from which every trace of Him seems to have vanished, and asks why he has been forsaken, and still obeys.

As a Christian virtue, gratitude will shape not only our deeds but also our emotions, feelings, and passions.

Nevertheless, since the development of such virtue is a journey that never ends in this life, there must for all of us be moments when we can feel no gratitude to God or to others – and yet ought to respond with grateful conduct.

Gratitude is an obligation. There is a good bit more to be said, but we should not leave this unsaid nor should we forget it at any step along the way. It is our duty to thank, praise, serve, and obey God – whether we feel like it or not. That, indeed, is one of the reasons for liturgy. It gives us the fitting word which we, subject in our lives to the law of undulation, might not find within our passing moods and feelings. And it is our duty to serve the neighbor. Many people depend on us. Directly or indirectly we meet the needs of many. No doubt it is best if we do so with a glad and willing spirit. But even if the spirit is not willing – or if the spirit is willing but the flesh is just too tired – it is a duty to serve those neighbors even as we have been served. We do many things for others which it is hard to do spontaneously and gratefully – meet budgets, attend meetings, wash dishes, care for elderly people grown senile, teach for the hundredth time the most simple and basic truth, feed babies in the middle of the night. There are times when little of this is or can be done solely because we are moved by a grateful spirit. We do it because we ought, even when the duty has lost all relish. There is more to the Christian life than this, but not less.

Gratitude Is an Obligation, But . . .

We need not think very long about gifts – not just God's gifts to us, but our own to each other – in order to realize that it is too simple just to say that receiving a gift obligates the recipient to show gratitude in return. If that were all there were to say, a gift would be a kind

of moral strait jacket which left little room for freedom
or spontaneity in the Christian life. Perhaps, of course,
there is less place for freedom than we would like. That
is better decided when we have finished.

We should notice, however, the way in which
Luther describes the gratitude which, he says, we are
"bound" to offer God in return for his blessings. We are
"to thank, praise, serve, and obey him." All important
words to be sure, but words into which we must pour
specific content. That content may be as different as our
lives and selves are different. Some may decide to serve
God by tracing backward Luther's own steps and adopt-
ing the monastic life. That choice is not for others, however, who may already have taken vows of another sort.
Some of us, affirming with the psalmist that the tracks
of God's chariot drip with fatness, may believe that a
proper response to his gifts of food and drink involves
doing without those gifts on certain days, or, in order to
share that gift with the hungry, doing without (let us
say) meat several days each week. Others may prefer to
send their check to one of the many organizations seeking to feed the world's hungry people without denying
themselves chicken, hamburger, or an occasional pork
chop. Some of us, deeply moved by the divine affirmation of our own life, may find ourselves unable to use
force aimed in any way at harming or killing another
human being. Others of us, equally moved by God's affirmation of our own life, may find ourselves moved to help
neighbors in need, even by the use of force.

Examples of this general point are endless. If God's
gifts make us duty bound to show gratitude in return, it
is seldom the case that this gratitude must be shown in
any particular way. Christians are not called to be Ralph
Nader to their neighbors, specifying in precise detail the
shape their grateful response to God ought to take.
Grateful Christians are to thank, praise, serve, and obey
God – in countless ways which are fitting and appropri-

ate in their lives. Thus, the obligation of gratitude need not destroy all freedom and spontaneity in the Christian life, nor need it turn us into moral imperialists who are quite certain that gratitude to the Giver of life obligates us all to buckle our seat belts.

Although the obligation of gratitude may be universal, we cannot "universalize" the ways in which it is shown or lived. Our free decisions will give shape – particular shape peculiar to our life and self – to our gratitude. We should note, in passing, that this sort of freedom does not apply to everything Christians do. There are, I think, duties which admit of no exceptions. Those who – in the name of freedom, spontaneity, and love – think otherwise will have to help the rest of us see how they would justify exceptions to our duty not to engage in forcible intercourse, or our duty not to dispose of those whose mental or physical disabilities would make them burdensome to the rest of us. One of the surest signs of the moral chaos of our time is that the duties which should be universalized are not, and those which should not be are. It is, I am afraid, not at all uncommon to find people who suspect that there are many exceptions to our duty to protect the life of the retarded but who simultaneously believe that all of us ought always buckle our seat belts.

It should be clear therefore that I hold no brief for the view that freedom alone characterizes the Christian life, if by that one means that all our duties have exceptions determined by the situation. I do believe, however, that even though we are "duty bound" to be grateful for God's gifts, we may often choose the ways in which this gratitude will take shape in our lives. Hence, a life characterized by gratitude is stamped at least as deeply by freedom as by obligation.

Thus far I have concerned myself mainly with the freedom. Can we say anything about the obligation? Paul Camenisch has suggested that a grateful response to a gift will involve both *grateful conduct* toward the giver and *grateful use* of the gift.[5] Neither of these need destroy freedom in the grateful life. Camenisch notes that the possible ways to demonstrate grateful conduct toward the giver "are legion, ranging from a simple 'thank you' to dedicating one's life to serving the donor" (p. 9). The requirement of grateful use may seem to restrict our freedom more. Camenisch writes:

> Would not most persons readily agree that I had committed a morally censurable violation if, having told my old philosophy professor that I was grateful for the gift of a rare edition of Kant's works, I then gave them to a paper recycling drive? . . . Similarly, could we not easily agree that great-great-grandmother's silver service given into my hands by my mother is not to be used for chemistry experiments, or that a medical education supported by donations from my low-income doctorless Appalachian village is not to be used to make me rich in the big over-doctored city? (p. 9)

Camenisch seems correct to suggest that if we acted in these ways we would have failed in a moral obligation which calls for grateful use of gifts received. It is, however, possible to complicate matters a little.

Suppose I give the rare edition of Kant's works to a genuine scholar (someone who positively revels in pondering the antinomies into which reason falls when it peers beyond its limits). Have I misused my professor's gift? Or what if, knowing that I will never again look at *Religion Within the Limits of Reason Alone*, much less the *Critique of Pure Reason*, I sell this rare edition in order to take my wife on a trip to Germany (including, of course, Königsberg)—a trip she richly deserves but which we could pay for in no other way? Would my old philosophy professor approve? And if he disapproves, does that show I have failed in my obligation of "grateful use" or that he did not really give freely?

To be a little less frivolous and come closer to the

sort of problem over which one might agonize, suppose I am that doctor whose medical education was financed in part by the poor townspeople of the village in which I grew up. Not to go back as their doctor because I prefer becoming rich "in the big over-doctored city" would probably bespeak a failure in my obligation to use their gift gratefully. I suspect, though, that such choices are usually more difficult. Probably when I left that community to study medicine I intended nothing other than to return as a physician in the community. But their gift has broadened my horizons. I have discovered not just new pleasures but also new talents and abilities which I possess. I have come to believe that these talents suit me best for a different calling – that, for example, I am best suited to work in a teaching hospital connected with a large university. This is the sort of choice people really face, and when considering it we are, I think, less certain what grateful use of such a gift may require. With respect to gratitude in particular we may say what G. H. von Wright said of virtue in general: "The path of virtue is never laid out in advance."[6]

The obligation of gratitude, therefore, even while it binds us, permits us a good measure of freedom. Even when our circumstances in life are very similar, we need not enact our gratitude in similar ways. Two children grow up with loving parents in upper-middle-class households and receive the gift of a Princeton education. Both have talents and temperaments which suit them for government service. One becomes an undersecretary in the State Department, the other spends his life designing scenery for theatrical productions. Similar circumstances, similar gifts moved by similar parental intentions, quite *dis*similar responses. But both children may be grateful, and both responses may enact their gratitude. Gratitude is not simply a matter of doing or failing to do our duty – though it is that. Our character is shaped not by a simple decision to obey or disobey a rule but by *how* we enact our gratitude. The possibilities are beyond numbering. The obligation of gratitude, even while binding us, permits that kind of freedom.

Gratitude Is a Peculiar Obligation

"There are obligations and debts which of their very nature cannot be adequately fulfilled and discharged."[7] To think through this sentence of Josef Pieper's is to discover a deeper sense in which we may hesitate simply to term gratitude an obligation.

Consider a passage from Aristotle's *Nicomachean Ethics*. In his famous discussion of friendship Aristotle notes that the structure of friendships will differ depending on whether the friends are (in certain ways) equal or unequal. He notes a feature which must characterize friendship between *un*equals.

> The person who has profited . . . must give honor in return, for in giving that he gives what it is possible for him to give. Friendship demands the possible; it does not demand what the giver deserves. In some cases, in fact, it is impossible to make the kind of return which the giver deserves, for instance, in the honors we pay to the gods and to our parents. Here no one could ever make a worthy return, and we regard a man as good if he serves them to the best of his ability. (VIII, 14)

In certain cases, Aristotle seems to suggest, the "obligation" of gratitude breaks through the categories of obligation-language. There are gifts for which no suitable return is possible, instances in which we cannot "make the kind of return which the giver deserves." Hence, to think of such relationships – to one's parents, or to God – simply in terms of an exchange of gift and gratitude will only indicate that we have missed something in the relationship. We should give what it is possible for us to give but should not imagine that in so doing we have somehow made an adequate return which fulfills an obligation of gratitude.

There may even be a sense in which it is true to say of *any* gift that it can never be fully repaid. There is in the giving a kind of ungrounded initiative which cannot be completely present in any act of grateful response. The recipient, even the truly grateful recipient, can never be the primal giver in this relationship. Paul Camenisch makes the point well.

> The recipient has an obligation to make appropriate return. But the donor had no such obligation and so acted with a freedom and spontaneity that is forever beyond the recipient in relation to this donor. This is a kind of moral advantage that can never be erased by the value of a return gift. Thus an attempt at complete repayment reflects the initial recipient's insensitivity to this dimension of the donor's act and to its ineradicable nature. (pp. 12f.)

It seems, therefore, that to think of duties which can be fulfilled through particular grateful deeds may be to deceive ourselves. We miss something when we try to repay a gift too completely and too promptly. Were gratitude simply an obligation to repay a gift it would be hard to explain why we feel that such attempts at prompt and complete repayment are morally deficient. But gratitude is not simply a duty. It involves a willingness to remain in debt even when we make return to the giver. To be grateful is gladly and willingly to remain needy. Seen from this angle, an attempt to think of gratitude only in terms of duty and obligation is really an attempt to protect ourselves.

Some gifts can never be repaid; perhaps none can be. This suggests something important about our relation not just to God but to each other. Our common life

together cannot fail to be somewhat harsh and alienating if we think of it simply in terms of obligations, justice, and rights. Already more than twenty years ago
Paul Tournier noted this, writing of young people who
are

> profoundly unhappy because they have lost a sense of
> gratitude. They can speak only of rights. Health is a
> right and sickness a frustration of this right. Healing, so
> quick now thanks to our antibiotics, is no longer a gift
> from God. Happiness is a right. Since no one achieves it,
> despite all our modern conveniences, everyone is the vic-
> tim of a frustration complex. No gift can bring joy to the
> one who has a right to everything.[8]

If today our common life in society is, as many observers
seem to think, a life lacking shared purpose and commitment – a life, that is, with little in common – perhaps at
least a part of the problem is this: We have understood
that common life largely in terms of rights and entitlements, in terms of the language of obligation, and not
in terms of a virtue like gratitude. What a terrible misunderstanding this could be if it should be true that
"there are obligations and debts which of their very
nature cannot be adequately fulfilled and discharged."

Our common life is an intricate web of relationships
in which giving and receiving go on constantly. We are
indebted to each other in countless ways. Some of these
debts are of the sort that can never be repaid. Perhaps
all of them are of this sort. Some debts must, of course,
be paid as best we can. Justice is and will remain a fundamental political good. Nevertheless, what if it is true
to say that "the world cannot be kept in order through
justice alone"?[9] A frantic attempt to keep all obligations
balanced in our common life will inevitably result in a
harsh, abrasive, and alienating world – a world in which
none of us is willing to be needy, in which all claim their
rights all the time, in which we all want to be equal in

our entitlements. Such a life is possible, but it is not a life which can have too much in the way of common purpose or common good. We therefore face a choice: Either we should stop bemoaning the loss of community and common purpose in our society, or we should learn to talk not just the language of rights and duties but also the language of virtue.

One example may put some flesh on the bones of this rather abstract argument. In discussing those obligations which by "their very nature cannot be adequately fulfilled and discharged," Josef Pieper offers the example of *pietas*, piety.[10] Echoes of this idea still remain in our talk of filial piety. *Pietas* refers to the parent-child relation and understands it as a bond in which the parents' gifts can never be repaid by the child. But who today wishes to understand the bond in this way? Parents who did not abort a child known to have some deformities while in the womb may find themselves in court defending against a charge of "wrongful life." And a perfectly healthy child may still feel that, having been given no choice about the gift of life, he need show no gratitude but may simply accept the beneficence of his parents not as beneficence but as his entitlement. Parents may come to think similarly of their children. They may see them not as members of their family for whom they gladly expend themselves but as objects of rational, economic calculation. To have a child at a time inconvenient for them, to have a child with mental or physical disabilities which they had not intended, perhaps even to have a girl when they wanted a boy – all this may come to seem a burden imposed on them, not a gift of life which they gladly offer. In such circumstances the family comes to be seen as a small political arena in which we talk not of gifts and gratitude but of entitlements and obligations. Along the way we may suddenly wonder what is common and shared in the life of this family. Again, therefore, perhaps we must learn to make a choice: Either we should be hesitant about hopping on the next "children's rights" bandwagon which comes along, or we must not bemoan the loss of common life in our families.

Some obligations and debts cannot by their very nature be fulfilled. It follows that we miss something important if we think of them simply as duties. This is especially true with respect to the relation between creature and Creator. Josef Pieper writes:

> *Before* any subsequent claim is made by men, indeed even before the mere possibility of such a human claim arises, comes the fact that man has been made a gift by God (of his being) such that his nature cannot ever "make it good," discharge it, "deserve" it , or return it again. Man can never say to God: We are even.[11]

Here at least we need to see that the gratitude for which a gift calls is not merely an obligation needing to be properly discharged. The language of virtue recognizes gratitude as an obligation which shatters the boundaries of our usual talk about duties; for gratitude is finally not a duty to be discharged but an attitude which must pervade and shape the whole of life. Pieper, a Roman Catholic philosopher, speaks language the Reformers would applaud when he nicely juxtaposes two passages from Luke's Gospel.[12] How mistaken an understanding of the gratitude creatures owe their Creator would it be to say with the Pharisee, "I fast twice a week. I give tithes of all that I possess" (Luke 18:12) – as if our situation were simply that of a person duty bound to repay a debt. Rather, gratitude as a virtue which pervades and shapes the whole of life may lead us, when we have done "all those things that are commanded," to say "we are unprofitable servants" (Luke 17:10).

Having pressed the matter this far, however, we must recognize a difficulty to which this analysis gives rise. There are, I have said, obligations which can never be discharged. Never could we say to God: We are even. How then shall we respond to a statement like the following?

> The good gift relation does not lock the recipient into the position of inferior, dependent, subordinate which would restrict rather than enhance the recipient's capacity to act as a free, autonomous agent. The good gift does not so overwhelm the recipient that the recipient is kept bound to the donor by indebtedness and is thus rendered unable to become a donor in return, or a donor to others.[13]

Perhaps it is not surprising that creatures sometimes rail against their Creator, that they rage against being locked into an inferior and dependent position. Perhaps it is also no surprise that children sometimes rebel against their parents, that they are reluctant to understand the relationship as one placing them under an obligation of gratitude which can never be discharged.

Up to this point we have considered two ways in which the obligation of gratitude is something more than just a duty. We noted, first, that as an obligation it leaves us free to fulfill it in countless ways, that our way need be no one else's and no one else's way need be ours. And, second, I have suggested that once we see that at least some gifts can never be repaid (and that perhaps none can), we may recognize that gratitude is something more than just a duty; it is a way of life. But the problem we have just raised points to a more difficult issue. If gifts create obligations of gratitude, if some gifts even lock us into permanent gratitude, should we begin to wonder whether gifts are really good for us? If gifts call for gratitude in return, this very call can threaten the genuineness of the gift. A gift is intended to set the recipient free to flourish in various ways; yet, insofar as it binds, it may do the opposite. And if it permanently binds — if a point never comes when we can say, "we are even"—then the problem is still more acute. Can we really say that a gift requires gratitude without destroying its character as *gift*? To this question we now turn.

Gratitude Is a Virtue

Let me begin with an example culled from one of the most important sources for ethical research—the "Dear Abby" column in the newspaper. I have in my files the following letter:

> DEAR ABBY: Last week my sister-in-law had a garage sale, and right out front was displayed the gift my husband and I had given her last Christmas! It had never been used and was sold for less than half of what we paid for it. (I would have bought it, but someone else got to it first.)
>
> My husband said it was hers to do whatever she pleased with it and I was stupid and oversensitive to give it a second thought.
>
> What do you think?—HURT

To which Abby responded as follows:

> DEAR HURT: Your husband is right when he says that the gift was hers to do with whatever she pleased. But he's wrong to label you "stupid and oversensitive" to give it a second thought. Your sister-in-law was the insensitive and stupid one for having offered your gift at a garage sale that you were apt to attend.

Unlike some cases we might encounter in "Dear Abby," this strikes me as an interesting and plausible one. There is a good bit to be learned from it.

Abby agrees that the gift was "hers to do with whatever she pleased." That is, if it's really a gift, there can't be strings attached. It is hard to deny the recipient a good measure of freedom to do as he or she will with a gift. Abby doesn't want to take that back. She affirms that freedom and even seems to think it would be quite all right to get rid of the gift – as long as the giver is happily ignorant of this. Any parents who have received fourteen pictures from a child on their birthday, and again at Christmas, and again on Valentine's Day will appreciate Abby's affirmation of the recipient's freedom. Nice as those drawings are, one runs out of things to do with them or space to keep them. Gifts should not be burdens. Recipients must in some way remain free. Abby's solution – to use terminology we discussed earlier – is that the recipient must demonstrate grateful *conduct* toward the giver but need not demonstrate grateful *use* of the gift. She can get rid of the gift but not in such a way as to hurt or embarrass the giver.

There is another interesting aspect to Abby's answer. The sister-in-law *was* insensitive to dispose of the gift in the way she did. As a third party to the situation Abby seems entitled to judge the sister-in-law in a way that the woman who gave the gift is not entitled. For the giver to judge that the recipient has been ungrateful comes close to taking back the "gift character" of the gift. If I give you a gift and then condemn you for ingratitude, my criticism suggests that the gift was not really free, that I was seeking to bind you to some return. It suggests, that is, that I did not intend to set you free by my gift. Hence, there is always something a little suspect about complaining that our gifts have not been met with grateful return. Third parties can make that judgment, and from their point of view it may make sense to think of gratitude as an obligation. But the giver cannot regard gratitude as a duty – not without poisoning the gift. Nor can the recipient. If I think myself obligated to show gratitude for your gift, I do not really experience it as gift. I am not set free by it. And any gratitude I show will be only an isolated deed of gratitude, not an expression of my character and the way of life to which I am committed. Third parties may make judgments about obligations of gratitude, but if givers and receivers do so, their relationship must necessarily be altered in important ways.

One more point is worth noting before we leave "Dear Abby" in peace. We have said that the giver should not demand or even expect gratitude in return for a gift; otherwise the gift is poisoned. Abby essentially agreed, we may recall, but she also insisted (contrary to the husband's view) that her correspondent was not "stupid and oversensitive" to be hurt by what had been done with her gift. We do well to listen to Abby here; for what I have said up to his point is open to a fatal misunderstanding. Whatever third parties may say, the giver cannot, I have insisted, require gratitude for his gift. How easy – and how destructive of our humanity – it would be to move from this truth to the view that we are wrong to be hurt when our gifts elicit no grateful response. We are Christians, not Stoics. This means at least that we are glad to acknowledge our dependence upon each other, that we do not believe the good life can be lived by retreating into the self and hardening ourselves against hurts. Our ideal is not invulnerability. Parents would be wrong to *demand* gratitude of their children – to turn that gratitude into an obligation. But if children are ungrateful and parents are not hurt, we may wonder how deeply they were committed to being parents. We are needy beings, in need of gratitude from those to whom we give much, and we can deny this truth only at the risk of our humanity.

We have learned a lot from "Dear Abby": that genuine gifts must set the recipient free; that though third parties may judge gratitude to be a duty, givers and receivers cannot think in those terms; that when gratitude is not shown us we quite naturally and appropriately are hurt. These observations may help us clarify *in thought* the fundamental tension which is always present when we give gifts. We may see more clearly that a gift, though intended to set us free, may become a burden. But to clarify in thought is not to remove from life. Giving which really liberates and receiving which is spontaneously grateful do not speak the language of obligation but of love. If gratitude is to be experienced not just as a duty but as a virtue which informs the whole of Christian life, both givers and receivers must be shaped by that self-giving spirit which is the fundamental form of Christian love. What we seek is not simply a right doing – appropriate gifts and grateful responses. What we seek is right being and right relationships. This suggests that it may be mistaken to concentrate – as I have for the most part done – solely upon the response of gratitude. How can gratitude be real until the gift is real?

One of Jesus' *a fortiori* arguments in the gospels begins, "If you then, who are evil, know how to give good gifts to your children . . ." (Matt. 7:11). But do we? Do we know how to give good gifts? Are we able to give gifts that set others free? Or do our gifts invariably burden them with obligations? All we need do is reflect upon the bond between parents and children to realize how seldom we succeed in giving good gifts to our children. Paul Tournier has observed:

> The good-night kiss is the most vital gift, provided it is not used as a reward which the child has to earn by good behavior, or even made subject to humble excuses for some folly committed during the day. Here we touch a subtle and all-important problem: To the child the conditional gift signifies a conditional love . . . . For then the gift as a sign of love appears to him to be a sign which he must earn not to say buy.[14]

The conditional gift signifies a conditional love. Can we give unconditionally?

Few people have managed to describe such unconditional love more powerfully than Søren Kierkegaard. In his *Works of Love* Kierkegaard suggests that the greatest love one person could show another would be to care for the other in such a way that it would be true to say, "he stands alone – by my help." And Kierkegaard continues,

> There are many writers who employ dashes on every occasion of thought-failure, and there are also those who use dashes with sensitivity and taste. But a dash has truly never been used more significantly than in the little sentence above . . . . For in this little sentence the infinity of thought is contained in the most profound way, the greatest contradiction overcome. He stands alone – this is the highest; he stands alone – nothing else do you see. You see no aid or assistance, no awkward bungler's hand holding on to him any more than it occurs to the person himself that someone has helped him. No, he stands alone – by another's help. But his help is hidden, . . . it is hidden behind a dash.[15]

To hide behind the dash. That is a moving description of unconditional giving which intends and achieves the freedom of the recipient. Such a gift would be good for us. Such giving, were we capable of it, might elicit genuine gratitude in return.

A gift, when it is a gift, intends to set us free. But gifts, insofar as they obligate us, are often experienced as burdens. This tension between gift and gratitude can be removed by no ethical theory, however perceptive. It can only be lived. But if not removed, it can be overcome by an act – a gift of which all our gifts are but pale imitations. If our creed had only a first article, we might assert this with less confidence. We confess, however, that the author of our being, who has rightful authority over us and whom we are "bound to thank, praise, serve, and obey" has not been content simply to assert that authority. He has chosen to give still more unconditionally, to give himself, to lay aside all claims to authority and live among us. This gift has set us free – even to renounce the Giver and crucify him. And to that his response in turn is not to accuse us of failing in an obligation of gratitude; his response is simply to offer himself anew, to carry the cross, to be one of us even as he woos us.

For us, in turn, it is both our duty and our delight at all times, in all places, and in countless ways to give thanks. It is our duty; we *ought* to show him gratitude. But it is also our delight, and no one whose life and character have been shaped by the story of this gift will imagine that obligation language is sufficient to depict our response. There are times when an obligatory gratitude is the best we can manage, and he is pleased to receive it. There are also moments, even if rare, when this story of "his boundless love toward us" so shapes us that our hearts are "warmed and kindled with gratitude to God and a desire to use all these blessings to his glory and praise." And shall we not say that for these moments in particular – these brief moments when we approach not just right doing but right being – we should be grateful?

Epilogue: A Meditation on Matthew 18:21-35

The ungrateful servant failed the test. He failed to respond with gratitude when his life was graced with the master's gift. To live in that master's kingdom was to live by the rule that gifts call for gratitude, and the servant didn't really desire such a life in such a kingdom. What could the master do to help him, to help one unwilling to see or adopt a rule of life characterized by gratitude? Maybe nothing. Maybe the master could do nothing for this servant.

But Jesus' parable does not suggest that the master's hands were, so to speak, tied by the ingratitude of the servant. The master in the story certainly finds something to do. He hands the wicked servant over to the torturers. Here gifts seem to come to an end, forgiveness reaches its limit. And this, Jesus says, is what the heavenly Father is like.

Can this be the last word about God? Can it be true that when his gifts do not elicit gratitude he hands the wicked servant over to the torturers – there to remain until the last penny of the debt is paid? Indeed, it is true. This is in truth the very last word about God. For whom does the Father hand over to the torturers? Is it not his own Son? Is it not Jesus who, though he was rich, yet for our sakes became a debtor? He is the one the Father hands over. He it is whom the Father will not release until the debt is paid.

This is the mystery of grace, of a gift which demands and requires nothing in return, not even gratitude. This gift of God is really a gift, perhaps the only real gift ever given. It is not cheap, but it is free. It cannot be cheap; for its price is, as Luther says in his explanation of the second article of the creed, "the holy precious blood and innocent suffering and death" of the Son of the Father. But it is really free – the gift of which even our best gifts are but halting imitations. Which is why one of the ancient prayers of the Church begins: "O God, you declare your almighty power *chiefly* in showing mercy and pity." This God, the Father of this Son, is the One who now says to us: freely you have received, freely give.[16]

Notes

1. Thinking about Virtue

1. Alasdair MacIntyre, *After Virtue: A Study in Moral Theory* (Notre Dame, Ind.: University of Notre Dame Press, 1981). In the paragraphs that follow page references to this book will be included in the body of the text.

2. Josef Pieper, *Scholasticism: Personalities and Problems of Medieval Philosophy* (New York: McGraw-Hill, 1964).

3. Josef Pieper, *The Four Cardinal Virtues* (Notre Dame, Ind.: University of Notre Dame Press, 1966), p. xii.

4.. G. H. von Wright, *The Varieties of Goodness* (London: Routledge & Kegan Paul, 1970), p. 148.

5. Ibid., p. 145.

6. William Frankena, *Ethics* (Englewood Cliffs, N. J. : Prentice-Hall, 1963), p. 52.

7. Von Wright, p. 139.

8. Michael Oakeshott, *Rationalism in Politics and Other Essays* (London: Methuen, 1962), pp. 7ff.

9. Stanley Hauerwas, *A Community of Character: Toward a Constructive Christian Ethic* (Notre Dame, Ind.: University of Notre Dame Press, 1981), p. 115.

10. James D. Wallace, *Virtues and Vices* (Ithaca, N.Y.: Cornell University Press, 1978), p. 46.

11. Philippa Foot, *Virtues and Vices and Other Essays in Moral Philosophy* (Berkeley: University of California Press, 1978), pp. 7f.

12. Dietrich Bonhoeffer, *Prisoner for God: Letters and Papers from Prison* (New York: Macmillan, 1958), p. 27.

13. Hauerwas, p. 115.

14. Ibid., pp. 114f.

15. Roger Wertheimer, "Understanding the Abortion Argument," in *The Rights and Wrongs of Abortion*, ed. Mar-

shall Cohen, Thomas Nagel, and Thomas Scanlon (Princeton, N. J.: Princeton University Press, 1974), p. 47.

16. Von Wright, p. 147; Foot, p. 8

17. Peter Geach, *The Virtues* (Cambridge: The University Press, 1977), p. 18. See also Wallace, p. 10.

18. Foot, p. 10.

19. Ibid., p. 11.

20. See Pieper, *The Four Cardinal Virtues*, pp. 162ff.

21. Foot, p. 9.

22. Bernard Williams, "Utilitarianism and Moral Self-Indulgence," in *Contemporary British Philosophy*, ed. H. D. Lewis (London: George Allen & Unwin, 1976), pp. 306–321.

23. C. S. Lewis, *Surprised by Joy: The Shape of My Early Life* (New York: Harcourt, Brace & World, 1956), p. 192.

24. Waldo Beach and H. Richard Niebuhr, eds., *Christian Ethics: Sources of the Living Tradition* (New York: Ronald Press, 1955), pp. 147ff.

25. Ibid., p. 149.

26. Robert Meagher, *Augustine: An Introduction* (New York: Harper Colophon Books, 1979), p. 58.

27. Ibid., p. 108.

28. An earlier version of this chapter was delivered as one of the Thomas F. Staley lectures at Valparaiso University in January 1982. It was later published in *The Cresset*, 45 (March 1982), pp. 11–18, under the title: "Exploring the Meaning of Virtue: New Reflections on an Old Word."

2. The Tradition of Virtue

1. J. G. A. Pocock, "Political Ideas as Historical Events: Political Philosophers as Historical Actors," in *Political Theory and Political Education*, ed. Melvin Richter (Princeton, N. J.: Princeton University Press, 1980), p. 139.

2. *Four Cardinal Virtues* (Notre Dame, Ind.: University of Notre Dame Press, 1964).

3. *Belief and Faith* (New York: Pantheon Books, 1963).

4. *About Love* (Chicago: Franciscan Herald Press, 1974).

5. *Über die Hoffnung* (Munich: Kösel-Verlag, 1961).

6. *Hope and History* (New York: Herder and Herder, 1969).

7. Pieper, *The Four Cardinal Virtues,* p. xii.

8. Pieper, *Auskunft Über die Tugenden* (Zurich: Verlag der Arche, 1970), pp. 9f.

9. Ibid., p. 10.

10. Pieper, *Belief and Faith,* pp. 60f.

11. Sir Arthur Conan Doyle, *The Complete Sherlock Holmes,* Vol. 2 (Garden City, N. Y.: Doubleday, 1930) p. 1058.

12. Charles Williams, *The Descent of the Dove: A Short History of the Holy Spirit in the Church* (Grand Rapids, Mich.: Eerdmans, 1939), p. 108.

13. Pieper, *The Four Cardinal Virtues,* p. 69.

14. Ibid., p. 124.

15. Ibid., p. 125.

16. Pieper, *The Silence of Saint Thomas* (New York: Pantheon Books, 1957), pp. 19f.

17. Alasdair MacIntyre, *After Virtue: A Study in Moral Theory* (Notre Dame, Ind.: University of Notre Dame Press, 1981), p. 145.

18. Iris Murdoch, *The Sovereignty of Good* (London: Routledge & Kegan Paul, 1970), p. 84.

19. John Finnis, *Natural Law and Natural Rights* (Oxford: The Clarendon Press, 1980), p. 31.

20. Pieper, *The Silence of Saint Thomas,* p. 96.

21. Ibid., p. 69.

22. Pieper, *The Four Cardinal Virtues,* p. 20.

23. Ibid., p. 5.

24. Ibid., p. 21.

25. Ibid., p. 32.

26. Cf. the comment of Alasdair MacIntyre in *After Virtue*: "For Kant one can be both good and stupid; but for Aristotle stupidity of a certain kind precludes goodness" (p. 145).

27. John Baillie, *A Diary of Private Prayer* (New York: Charles Scribner's Sons, 1949), p. 49.

28. See Pieper, *The Four Cardinal Virtues,* pp. 35-40. The paragraphs that follow discuss these pages, and any citations not otherwise identified can be found within these pages.

29. Josef Pieper, "On the Christian Idea of Man," *The Review of Politics* 11 (January 1949), p. 15.

30. See Pieper, *About Love,* pp. 116-122. The paragraphs

that follow discuss these pages, and any citations not otherwise identified can be found within these pages.

31. See Pieper, *The Four Cardinal Virtues*, pp. 134-141. The paragraphs that follow discuss these pages, and any citations not otherwise identified can be found within these pages.

32. Pieper, *The Four Cardinal Virtues*, p. 125.

33. Ibid., p. 123.

34. Ibid., p. 134.

35. James D. Wallace, *Virtues and Vices* (Ithaca, N. Y.: Cornell University Press, 1978), p. 52

36. Pieper, *The Four Cardinal Virtues*, p. 30.

37. Ibid., p. 26.

38. Josef Pieper, *Happiness and Contemplation* (London: Faber and Faber, 1959), pp. 55f. He identifies the commentator on the *Summa* as Bartholome de Medina.

39. Pieper, *Über die Hoffnung*, pp. 11ff.

40. Ibid., p. 21

41. Ibid., pp.72ff.

42. Ibid., p. 75.

43. Pieper, *The Four Cardinal Virtues*, pp. 147-152.

44. Ibid., p. 67.

45. Ibid., p. 147.

46. Ibid., p. 149.

47. William Frankena, *Ethics* (Englewood Cliffs, N. J.: Prentice-Hall 1963), p. 48.

48. Pieper, *Auskunft Über die Tugenden*, pp. 37f.

49. Donald Evans, *Struggle and Fulfillment: The Inner Dynamics of Religion and Morality* (Cleveland: Collins, 1979), p. 53

50. Alasdair MacIntyre, "Can Medicine Dispense with a Theological Perspective on Human Nature?" in *Knowledge, Value and Belief*, ed. Tristram Engelhardt, Jr. and Daniel Callahan. Vol. II in The Foundations of Ethics and Its Relationship to Science (Hastings-on-Hudson: The Institute of Society, Ethics, and the Life Science, 1977), pp. 26f.

51. Pieper, *Happiness and Contemplation*, pp. 35f.

52. Pieper, *The Four Cardinal Virtues*, p. 120.

53. Ibid., p. 120.

54. Pieper, *Hope and History*, p. 21.

55. Pieper, *Über die Hoffnung*, p. 46

56. Pieper, *Hope and History*, p. 91.

57. Ibid., p. 87.

58. MacIntyre, *After Virtue*, p. 204.

59. Pieper, *Happiness and Contemplation*, p. 97.

60. My thanks to a number of parties who helped make this chapter possible: to the National Endowment for the Humanities and Oberlin College's Research and Development Committee for their support with funds for travel; to Josef Pieper who, in November 1981, took time to talk with me about his life and work; to Paul Ramsey and Stanley Hauerwas, who commented helpfully on a first draft of this chapter; to the Thomas F. Staley Foundation which sponsored an earlier version of the chapter as one of the Staley Lectures at Valparaiso University in January 1982; and to my listeners on that occassion for their interest and response. An earlier version of this chapter, under the title "Josef Pieper – Explorations in the Thought of a Philosopher of Virtue," appeared in *The Journal of Religious Ethics*" (Spring 1983), 114-134.

3: Teaching Ethics and Shaping Character

1. References to a number of Plato's dialogues will be given in parentheses within the body of the text. Here I note the translations I will cite: (1) *Protagoras*, trans. C. C. W. Taylor (Oxford: Clarendon Press, 1976); (2) *Meno*, trans. W. K. C. Guthrie, in *The Collected Dialogues of Plato*, ed. Edith Hamilton & Huntington Cairns (New York: Bollingen Foundation, 1961): (3) *Theatetus*, trans. F. M. Cornford, in *The Collected Dialogues of Plato*; (4) *The Republic*, trans. Allan Bloom (New York: Basic Books, 1968); (5) *The Laws*, trans. Thomas L. Pangle (New York: Basic Books, 1980). (6) "Seventh Letter," trans. L. A. Post, in *The Collected Dialogues of Plato*. (Boston and New York: Houghton Mifflin, 1929), p. 130.

2. Frederick J. E. Woodbridge, *The Son of Apollo: Themes of Plato* (Boston and New York: Houghton Mifflin, 1929), p. 130.

3. Ibid., p. 127.

4. Werner Jaeger, *Paideia: The Ideals of Greek Culture*,

Vol. II, trans. Gilbert Highet (New York: Oxford University Press, 1943), p. 105.

5. Alasdair MacIntyre, *After Virtue: A Study in Moral Theory* (Notre Dame, Ind.: University of Notre Dame Press, 1981), pp. 8ff.

6. Robert E. Cushman, *Therapeia: Plato's Conception of Philosophy* (Chapel Hill: University of North Carolina Press, 1958), p. 35.

7. Iris Murdoch, *The Sovereignty of Good* (London: Routledge & Kegan Paul, 1970), p. 84.

8. For a helpful summary I have relied upon G. M. A. Grube, *Plato's Thought* (London: Methuen, 1935), p. 240.

9. Cushman (pp. 140ff.) suggests that the myth of the cave illumines three features of our human condition: (1) environment greatly influences ontological perception; (2) there is no cure for not seeing except seeing (no way to give moral knowledge to those who are not virtuous); and (3) our failure to know the good involves not just our intellectual but also our affective powers. The educational program of the *Republic* is intended to deal with all three.

10. MacIntyre, p. 114.

11. Stanley Hauerwas, *A Community of Character: Toward a Constructive Christian Ethic* (Notre Dame, Ind.: University of Notre Dame Press, 1981), p. 270, n. 7.

12. Woodbridge, p. 131.

13. Ibid., p. 142.

14. Ibid., p. 147.

15. Murdoch, p. 34.

16. Ibid., p. 52.

17. Ibid., p. 66.

18. Cushman, p. xix.

19. Jaeger, p. 66.

20. Peter Geach, *The Virtues* (Cambridge: at the University Press, 1977), p. 160.

21. James D. Wallace, *Virtues and Vices* (Ithaca, N. Y.: Cornell University Press, 1978), p. 77.

22. For a similar view, though one arrived at by a different chain of reasoning, see R. E. Allen, "The Socratic Paradox," *Journal of the History of Ideas* 12 (1960), 256-265. Consider, for example, Allen's concluding summary statement: "Virtue implies both grasp and capacity; but both are

rooted in a form of intuition so fundamental that it touches every corner of the self, an intuition which entails the complete integration of the personality. It follows that there is a dimension of meaning in the Socratic paradox which must remain dark and difficult to understand; for the paradox issues from a depth of experience which few have attained . . ." (p. 265).

23. Ep VII, 340b.

24. Richard Rorty, *Philosophy and the Mirror of Nature* (Princeton, N.J.: Princeton University Press, 1979). Rorty's thesis is, in fact, more wide-ranging than my description suggests. His attack is on the view that philosophy can serve as a "foundational" discipline for the rest of culture. I would not pretend to comment on Rorty's view of the role of philosophy but will leave that issue to those concerned about it. My focus will be restricted to one element of Rorty's case – that permanent, objective standards of moral truth cannot be found. An epistemological view similar to Rorty's has been applied specifically to morality by Jeffrey Stout in *The Flight from Authority* (Notre Dame, Ind.: university of Notre Dame Press, 1981). References to Rorty's book in the pages that follow will be given by page number in parentheses within the body of the text.

25. Rorty, pp. 365ff. The two styles seem quite similar to Oakeshott's distinction between didactic and contemplative styles in philosophy. Cf. Michael Oakeshott; Introduction to Hobbes's *Leviathan* (Oxford: Blackwell, 1955), p. xviii.

26. Josef Pieper, *The Silence of Saint Thomas* (New York: Pantheon Books, 1957), p. 96. Compare a similar statement from a Jewish thinker with a firm grip on the world as created: "The Torah, we are told, is both concealed and revealed, and so is the nature of all reality. All things are both known and unknown, plain and enigmatic, transparent and impenetrable. 'Hidden are the things that we see; we do not know what we see.' The world is both open and concealed, a matter of fact and a mystery. We know and do not know – this is our condition." Abraham Joshua Heschel, *God in Search of Man: A Philosophy of Judaism* (New York: Farrar, Straus & Cudahy, 1955), p. 59.

27. Michael Oakeshott, "The Idea of a University," *The Listener* 43 (1950), 424. Other citations of this article in the

next few paragraphs will be identified by page number in parentheses within the body of the text.

28. Allan Bloom, "Interpretive Essay," in *The Republic of Plato*, trans. Allan Bloom (New York: Basic Books, 1968), p. 410.

29. Josef Pieper, *Scholasticism: Personalities and Problems of Medieval Philosophy* (New York: McGraw-Hill, 1964), p. 155. Compare C. S. Lewis' remark in *Surprised by Joy* (New York: Harcourt, Brace & World, 1955) about a conversation between himself, Owen Barfield, and Dom Bede Griffiths. "Once, when he and Barfield were lunching in my room, I happened to refer to philosophy as 'a subject.' 'It wasn't a *subject* to Plato,' said Barfield, 'it was a way.' " (p. 225)

30. Woodbridge, p. 88.

31. Cushman, pp. 298ff.

32. Ibid., p. 300.

33. Ibid., p. 213.

4. Instructing the Conscience

1. D. H. Meyer, *The Instructed Conscience: The Shaping of the American National Ethic* (Philadelphia: University of Pennsylvania Press, 1972), p. xi.

2. Mark T. Lilla, "Ethos, 'Ethics,' and Public Service," *The Public Interest*, No. 63 (Spring 1981), p. 4.

3. Ibid., p. 13.

4. Iris Murdoch, *The Sovereignty of Good* (London: Routledge & Kegan Paul, 1970), p. 52.

5. Louis E. Raths, Merrill Harmin, Sidney B. Simon, *Values and Teaching: Working With Values in the Classroom*, 2nd ed. (Columbus, Ohio: Charles E. Merrill, 1978), p. 34.

6. Sidney B. Simon and Polly deSherbinin, "Values Clarification: It Can Start Gently and Grow Deep," *Phi Delta Kappan* 56 (June 1975), 682.

7. C. S. Lewis, *Mere Christianity* (New York: Macmillan, 1960), p. 146.

8. Simon and deSherbinin, p. 682.

9. Richard A. Baer, Jr., "Values Clarification as Indoctrination," *Educational Forum* 41 (January 1977), 155-165.

10. Ibid., pp. 160f.

11. Michael Scriven, "Cognitive Moral Education," *Phi Delta Kappan* 56 (June 1975), p. 692 (emphasis his).

12. *Nicomachean Ethics*, I, 4 (1095b).

13. Andrew Oldenquist, " 'Indoctrination' and Societal Suicide," *The Public Interest*, No. 63 (Spring 1981), p. 94.

14. Cf. the argument of C. S. Lewis, *The Abolition of Man* (New York: Macmillan, 1947), pp. 31ff.

15. *The Teaching of Ethics in Higher Education* (Hastings-on-Hudson, N. Y.: The Hastings Center, 1980), p. 54.

16. Richard Peters, *Authority, Responsibility and Education* (London: George Allen & Unwin, 1959), p. 90.

17. Lawrence Kohlberg, "Stages of Development as a Basis for Moral Education," in *Moral Education: Interdisciplinary Approaches*, ed. C. M. Beck, B. S. Crittenden, and E. V. Sullivan (Toronto: University of Toronto Press, 1971), p. 31.

18. Ibid., p. 34

19. More recently Kohlberg has noted that his research does not really support the existence of the sixth and highest stage – except as a position espoused for the most part by some who have done advanced study in moral philosophy! Nevertheless, for some reason the sixth stage always seems to remain in general descriptions of the theory. Cf. Thomas Lickona, "What Does Moral Psychology Have to Say to the Teacher of Ethics?" in *Ethics Teaching in Higher Education*, ed. Daniel Callahan and Sissela Bok (New York and London: Plenum Press, 1980), p. 107.

20. Lawrence Kohlberg, "Moral Stages and Moralization: The Cognitive-Developmental Approach," in *Moral Development and Behavior*, ed. Thomas Lickona (New York: Holt, Rinehart and Winston, 1976), p. 36.

21. Lawrence Kohlberg, "Education for Justice: A Modern Statement of the Platonic View," in *Moral Education: Five Lectures*, ed. Nancy F. Sizer and Theodore R. Sizer (Cambridge, Mass.: Harvard University Press, 1970), p. 57.

22. Lawrence Kohlberg, "A Reply to Owen Flanagan and Some Comments on the Puka-Goodpaster Exchange," *Ethics* 92 (April 1982), 516ff.

23. Kohlberg, "Education for Justice . . . ," p. 58.

24. Kohlberg, "Stages of Development . . . ," p. 42.

25. Ibid., pp. 42ff.

26. Kohlberg, "Education for Justice . . . ," p. 82. Over the years Kohlberg's approach to moral development has taken on more complexity. He now stresses the value not just of hypothetical discussions but of membership in "just communities" which foster communal attachment while seeking to operate by consensus. Cf. Joseph Reimer, "Moral Education: The Just Community Approach," *Phi Delta Kappan* 62 (March 1981), 485-487. Preliminary findings suggest that, though this approach does not stimulate more rapid progress through the several stages, it does influence student behavior – that is, it has an affective not just a cognitive effect. Reimer writes: "I interpret these preliminary findings to suggest that the discussion of moral dilemmas is still the most effective means of attaining the single goal of promoting student moral judgment. However, for those aiming for the more complex goals of promoting the application of moral reasoning to the life of the school, the just community approach may prove most promising" (p. 487). What is this except a recognition that Durkheim and his successors, who emphasized the importance of internalizing external norms in the development of moral behavior (not just reasoning), were on target? Reimer notes that Kohlberg first turned to this approach because of his reading of Durkheim and his acquaintance with educational systems in the Israeli kibbutz (p. 486).

27. Kohlberg, "Education for Justice . . . ," pp. 59f.

28. Kohlberg, "Stages of Development . . . ," p. 73. Of course, Kohlberg's caricature of the stories through which appropriate moral attitudes can be instilled suggests that either he has just missed the truth in these stories or he has read few really good stories for children. I am not certain which would be the more damning indictment.

29. Ibid., p. 47.

30. Lawrence Kohlberg, "From Is to Ought: How to Commit the Naturalistic Fallacy and Get Away with It in the Study of Moral Development," in *Cognitive Development and Epistemology*, ed. Theodore Mischel (New York and London: Academic Press, 1971), p. 183.

31. Kohlberg, "Moral Stages and Moralization . . . ," p. 32.

32. Lickona, "What Does Moral Psychology Have to Say . . . ?" p. 115.

33. Lewis, *The Abolition of Man*, p. 34.

34. I discuss some of the problems of universalizability in chapter three above. From a different angle, I have suggested that some of the tensions between particular attachments and universal obligations are not resolved as easily as Kohlberg might suggest in *Friendship: A Study in Theological Ethics* (Notre Dame, Ind.: University of Notre Dame Press, 1981).

35. Kohlberg, "From Is to Ought . . . ," p. 213.

36. Ibid.

37. Murdoch, p. 84.

38. R. S. Peters, "Moral Development: A Plea for Pluralism," in Mischel, ed., *Cognitive Development and Epistemology*, p. 262.

38. Craig R. Dykstra, *Vision and Character: A Christian Educator's Alternative to Kohlberg* (New York/Ramsey: Paulist Press, 1981).

40. Ibid., p. 59.

41. Kohlberg, "From Is to Ought . . . ," p. 213.

42. Ronald Duska and Mariellen Whelan, *Moral Development: A Guide to Piaget and Kohlberg* (New York: Paulist Press, 1975), p. 66.

43. Several authors have recently suggested that Kohlberg's theory is deficient in this assumption because his original longitudinal studies were carried out on a group composed exclusively of males – studies which led him to conclude that women, who tended to emphasize personal attachments and loyalties, often did not progress beyond stage three reasoning. Cf. Owen J. Flanagan, Jr., "Virtue, Sex, and Gender: Some Philosophical Reflections on the Moral Psychology Debate," *Ethics* 92 (April 1982), 499-512; and Carol Gilligan, *In A Different Voice: Psychological Theory and Women's Development* (Cambridge, Mass.: Harvard University Press, 1982).

44. E. M. Forster, "What I Believe," in *Two Cheers for Democracy* (London: Edward Arnold, [1951], rpt. 1972), p. 66.

45. Kohlberg, "Stages of Development . . . ," p. 71.

46. Kenneth E. Goodpaster, "Kohlbergian Theory: A

Philosophical Counterinvitation," *Ethics* 92 (April 1982) 497.

47. Spurious also in practice, one might add. Consider, for example, the description by one author of how this development theory might be applied to college students – a theory, we remember, which seeks neutrality among substantive moral positions and seeks to foster a natural dynamic within the student, not impose an alien value system. "Most students coming to college, for example, will be operating at the conventional level, Kohlberg's Stages 3 and 4. The task of the introductory ethics teacher will be to dislodge them from their unreflective conventional morality, to shake them loose from their unexamined assumptions and values. That kind of freeing up is one way to facilitate the transition from conventional to postconventional, principled morality . . . ." Lickona, "What Does Moral Psychology Have to Say . . . ?" p. 119.

5. The Examined Life Is Not Worth Leading

1. I am quoting from the Revised Standard Version.

2. Stanley Hauerwas, *Character and the Christian Life* (San Antonio: Trinity University Press, 1975), pp. 12ff.

3. Martin Luther, "Against Latomus," *Luther's Works*, Vol. 32 (Philadelphia: Fortress Press, 1958), pp. 133-260. Page references for citations will be noted in parentheses within the body of the text.

4. Nor is this merely the "introspective conscience" which it is fashionable to charge Luther with having foisted upon Western Christendom. In the same context Luther quotes St. Paul's, "I am not aware of anything against myself but I am not thereby acquitted" in support of his position ("Against Latomus," p. 190).

5. Luther also writes that God himself does not deny that these virtues are good. That is, taken by themselves and considered in isolation from the person as a whole, some of them merit praise. And, says Luther, God does indeed reward such virtues with temporal benefits ("Against Latomus," p. 225). This is interesting in that Luther here inverts the old problem of whether a good man can be harmed. One way to deal with the problem was to assert that, whatever a good man might suffer in this life, he was bound to be rewarded for

his virtues in the next. Luther suggests the opposite: Before God judgments are made upon selves, not upon their virtues taken in isolation. But in this life, before the world, God is content that such isolated virtues should have their reward.

6. Martin Luther, "Lectures on Galatians, 1535: Chapters 1-4," *Luther's Works*, Vol. 26 (St. Louis: Concordia Publishing House, 1963). Page references for citations will be noted in parentheses within the body of the text.

7. Werner Elert, *The Structure of Lutheranism* (St. Louis: Concordia Publishing House, 1962), p. 81.

8. For example, for consideration of an analogous problem in the theological ethic of Karl Barth, see William Werpehowski, "Command and History in the Ethics of Karl Barth," *The Journal of Religious Ethics* 9 (Fall 1981), 298-320.

9. Hauerwas, p. 16.

10. Ibid., p. 4.

11. Gerald Strauss, *Luther's House of Learning: Indoctrination of the Young in the German Reformation* (Baltimore and London: The Johns Hopkins University Press, 1978). Page references for citations will be noted in parentheses within the body of the text. In terms of an older but still important and influential generation of Luther scholarship, we could say that Strauss tends to support the claims of Ernst Troeltsch rather than Karl Holl: Lutheranism did not manage to shape a society. Before that could be done, Protestants would have to become more willing than early Lutherans were to commit themselves – as Catholics had – to the examined life.

12. An earlier version of this chapter, under the title "The Virtues: A Theological Analysis," is to appear in the volume *Virtue and Medicine*, edited by Earl E. Shelp, to be published by the D. Reidel Publishing Company.

6. It Killed the Cat

1. Leon R. Kass, " 'Making Babies' Revisited," *The Public Interest*, No. 54, (Winter 1979), pp. 59f.

2. C. S. Lewis, *The Magician's Nephew* (New York: Mac-

millan, 1955). References to *The Magician's Nephew* will be identified in parentheses within the body of the text.

3. Trans. Rex Warner (New York: New American Library, 1963), Mentor-Omega Book. Unidentified citations in the following paragraphs will come from *Confessions*, X, 35.

4. C. S. Lewis, *The Screwtape Letters* with *Screwtape Proposes a Toast* (New York: Macmillan, 1961), p. 56.

5. St. Augustine, *The City of God*, trans. Henry Bettenson (New York: Penguin Books, 1972), XXII, 24.

6. Robert E. Meagher, *Augustine: An Introduction* (New York: Harper Colophon Books, 1979). All citations in this paragraph can be found in pp. 192-196.

7. For a more precise delimitation of some "forbidden truths," see David H. Smith, "Scientific Knowledge and Forbidden Truths," *The Hastings Center Report*, December 1978, pp. 30-35.

8. St. Thomas Aquinas, *Summa Theologiae*, Blackfriars Edition (London: Eyre & Spottiswoode, 1972).

9. Ibid., pp. 192f.

10. Ibid., pp. 202f.

11. Josef Pieper, *The Four Cardinal Virtues* (Notre Dame, Ind.: University of Notre Dame Press, 1966), p. 200.

12. Smith, p. 33.

13. John Henry Cardinal Newman, *The Idea of a University* (Notre Dame, Ind.: University of Notre Dame Press, 1982). References to *The Idea of a University* will be identified within parentheses in the body of the text.

14. My thanks to David Smith and Paul Ramsey for their helpful criticisms of an earlier draft of this chapter.

7. The Virtue of Gratitude

1. *Large Catechism*, II, 19. See Theodore G. Tappert, ed., *The Book of Concord* (Philadelphia: Muhlenberg Press, 1959), p. 412.

2. *Large Catechism*, II, 23. See Tappert, p. 413.

3. *Large Catechism*, II, 24. See Tappert, p. 413.

4. Macmillan Paperbacks Edition (New York: Macmillan, 1961). All references and citations in the following paragraphs come from Letter VIII (pp. 36-39).

5. Paul Camenisch, "Gift and Gratitude in Ethics," *The Journal of Religious Ethics* 9 (Spring 1981), pp. 8ff. Further references to this article will be made by page numbers within parentheses in the body of the text.

6. G. H. von Wright, *The Varieties of Goodness* (London: Routledge & Kehan Paul, 1970), p. 145.

7. Josef Pieper, *The Four Cardinal Virtues* (Notre Dame, Ind.: University of Notre Dame Press, 1966), p. 110.

8. Paul Tournier, *The Meaning of Gifts* (Richmond, Va.: John Knox Press, 1963), pp. 31f.

9. Pieper, p. 104.

10. Ibid., pp. 107ff.

11. Ibid., p. 105.

12. Ibid., p. 107.

13. Camenisch, p. 29.

14. Tournier, pp. 23f.

15. Søren Kierkegaard, *Works of Love* (New York: Harper Torchbooks, 1964), pp. 256f.

16. This chapter was presented as an essay at the Continuing Education Conference for Lutheran Bishops and Presidents at Keystone, Colorado, in July 1983. It is to be published in a volume including the other essays presented on that occasion.